IT IS NOT IMPOSSIBLE!

Building a Business from ZERO
Using the *"Bulldozer Method"*

TIM MANSOUR

Copyright © 2017 Tim Mansour

All rights reserved. No part(s) of this book may be reproduced, distributed or transmitted in any form, or by any means, or stored in a database or retrieval systems without prior expressed written permission of the author of this book.

Paperback ISBN: 978-1-5356-0838-1
Hardcover ISBN: 978-1-5356-1015-5

Dedication

This book is dedicated to my mother, father, and older brother, Lt. Colonel Paul Mansour.

Joe and Isabel Mansour, my parents

Lt. Colonel Paul Joseph Mansour, my brother

Contents

Dedication iii
About Tim Mansour… 1
Chapter 1: What IS the "Bulldozer Method"? 3
Chapter 2: Where My Business Dreams Began 9
Chapter 3: The Ugly Truth Is Revealed! 15
Chapter 4: My Family, My Strength, My Faith and My Passion 17
Chapter 5: A New Day and a New Beginning! 27
Chapter 6: The Beginning of My Business Journey 31
Chapter 7: Giving My Dream a Name 37
Chapter 8: The Big Search! 39
Chapter 9: What a Great Day! 43
Chapter 10: Bigger & Better! 49
Chapter 11: Expanding to the Mountain 53
Chapter 12: Let's keep rolling… 57
Chapter 13: Gwinnett's Mega Club 61
Chapter 14: Club Business Operations and the Day-to-Day Grind .. 65
Chapter 15: Keep Your Eyes Wide Open! 67
Chapter 16: The Worst Three Years of My Life! 71
Chapter 17: Holding a Grudge OR Letting It Go! 75
Chapter 18: Tennis Anyone? 79
Chapter 19: Creative Money Management 83
Chapter 20: How to Weather the Storms of Your Business! . 87
Chapter 21: The Decision to Start Scaling Back the Business! 91
Chapter 22: The Best Part of My Life, My Children and My Wife! .. 93
Chapter 23: The Negotiation of My Life 99
Chapter 24: A New Plan for Collins Hill Athletic Club 105
Chapter 25: The next chapter of our life! 109

A Special Note of Gratitude 110

Comments from Family, Friends and Team Members 111

About Tim Mansour...

Tim Mansour is a prominent Georgia businessman, entrepreneur, real estate investor and philanthropist. He built and operated four Fitness International, Inc., Health Clubs and several offspring businesses for more than 30 years. He worked with thousands of employees, comprised of numerous family members and many friends during this time. He and his wife, Chrystal Williams Mansour, reside in Grayson, Georgia. Tim and his former wife, Cherry Reynolds Tolliver, have two adult children: Dr. Cory Mansour (married to Lauren Wilburn Mansour) and Haley Mansour Hightower (married to Terry Hightower). Tim and Chrystal currently own and operate Impact One Services.

- Self-employed for more than 30 years; managed 300 plus employees, at any given time, among a half-dozen businesses
- Owned and operated ten different businesses, which were sold over a period of time for a total of $10.8 million dollars
- Board member, Leadership Gwinnett "Glance Program," 2014
- President, American Heart Association Gwinnett, 2005
- *Georgia Trend* magazine "Georgia's Top 40 Business Leaders under 40," 1999
- Georgia Chamber of Commerce "Georgia Business Man of the Year," 1997
- Gwinnett Chamber of Commerce "Gwinnett Business Man of the Year," 1996
- Rockdale Chamber of Commerce "Jerry Barbee Small Business Person of the Year" finalist, 1996
- Member of Leadership Gwinnett, 1994
- *Gwinnett Magazine* readers voted Fitness International "Best in Gwinnett" fitness center for seven straight years, 1998–2004

Chapter 1

What IS the "Bulldozer Method"?

My motto: "Do whatever it takes to get the job done, as long as it's morally right!"

I always dreamed of owning a business. Getting started was not easy, especially when I literally started with zero! NO capital, NO investors, NO advisors and NO experience. My business vision started as one big dream, and as a 22-year-old, most people didn't really take me too seriously. I had to see and feel and taste my dream for myself. I coined the term *"the bulldozer method."* It was a metaphor for rolling over any obstacles that stifled my passion, and the determination needed to obtain my personal and professional goals. When I faced roadblocks, I visualized and learned to rethink, but never let them stop my dreams from becoming reality. I understood that to succeed in business, I had to approach many obstacles like a bulldozer. I also realized that I would need to dedicate most of my time and effort to my career. Somehow, I wanted it all. I wanted my dreams but I didn't want my family to take a backseat. I believed I could keep my loved ones close, and somehow maintain the drive to "bulldoze" my way past negative forces. This was never easy, but it was my goal.

I believe there are two types of business people; the ones with the blinders effect and the ones that have a pinball effect. For example, picture a race horse. Blinders are put on a race horse for a reason, to run straight to the finish line with no distractions. That fits best in my *bulldozer method* of thinking. You can adjust your blinders to see a bit more, but focus is a necessity. The second type of business person has a pinball effect. At first glance, it will seem like they are great multi-taskers. They are filled with ideas. They are excited. They run in many directions, but never quite make it to the finish line. Their ideas are usually great ones, but they become too much of a distraction. They tend to keep moving their finish line. That business person operates like a pinball machine, bouncing from idea-to-idea, but never meeting the actual goal.

Even early on, I learned to surround myself with positive-minded people. Not YES people, but people that had experience that I didn't have yet and that had experienced some success. You will learn, as I did, that it isn't how you handle things when all is going well but how you handle them when times are tough. I am proud that I have learned to make the best of bad situations, because, just like every business, there will be obstacles and tough times. I just kept telling myself that I had to be strong enough and smart enough to make my dream a reality. I had to feel as strong and mighty as a bulldozer. In no way is my mantra to be misconstrued as coming off as a "bully"—just the opposite. I was raised to respect those around me and I did. I questioned what didn't work and figured out another path. Sometimes that meant I needed help, sometimes it just appeared to me as an obvious choice. I can say to you, believe in yourself, and the nonbelievers will come around or eventually disappear!

Every part of you will be challenged during this ride to making your dream a reality. Mine has certainly been tested, repeatedly. I believe it shows us who we really are and that knowledge and growth are worth every second of the ride. So, enjoy this story of my journey and the precious lessons I learned along the way once the dust had settled…

My Life and Where It All Began…

I was born November 30, 1959 in Griffin, GA, just south of Atlanta. I was the middle child, with an older sister and brother and two younger brothers. We were close in every way. Literally, all five of us were born in six years. I had very busy parents. My mother worked at a Big Apple Grocery Store and my father was an insurance man with Coastal States Life Insurance Company. My four grandparents were all born in Lebanon, in Zahle` and Beirut, so I am of Lebanese descent.

We were poor, but we were very close growing up, and I could go on for hours telling stories about the adventures of being a Mansour.

When I was 14 years old, my dad received a promotion to management, moving us to Rome, GA. I started ninth grade at Coosa Junior High.

My Plan, God's Plan…

I was a C student at best, but a naturally good athlete. I began playing football, and was the only freshman on the varsity team. I lettered in football and baseball all four years in high school and also competed in wrestling, and track.

My goal at that time was to play for a Division-1 college in football or baseball. After my junior year, and more than 25 letters of athletic interest from colleges, my father and I made the decision that I should play football. While I was being recruited, I received several letters stating that if I had a good senior year and remained healthy, my percentages were extremely high of receiving a full scholarship from a Division-1 school. This was one of the first big goals in my life and I took it very seriously. I trained harder than ever before to get ready for my senior year of high school football. The first game of the season was against Model High School. At that time, Model was one of the weaker teams in our division. I had a conversation with Coach Leroy Jackson and he felt that, as a fullback, I was on track to having an outstanding game to start my senior year. I was pumped. The second play of the game was a life changer. I was hit hard while carrying the ball but rolled off, put the ball in my left hand, and was headed toward the corner. Once again, I was met with a hard tackle. I remember thinking that I did not want to hit the ground, but as I fell, I extended my right arm to catch myself and landed with all my weight on my thumb. A sharp pain shot up my arm. I grabbed my hand and was forced to leave the field. Our team trainer, Oscar, rushed over to me. Within seconds, he realized that my thumb was torn away from the joint. While holding my thumb in place, I asked him to tape my thumb, so I could return to the game. Back in the game, I'm ready for the very next play. Again, I carried the ball, gaining significant yardage, but once I was tackled and hit the ground, my thumb popped out of joint again. At that point, I was out. Our team doctor met Coach Jackson and me in the field house after the game and affirmed the diagnosis. I would need surgery to repair the damage. I was taken to Atlanta Medical Center, where Dr. Almond placed two pins in my thumb and wrist. I never played another high school football game. I remember thinking, okay, God, this isn't part of my plan.

After high school graduation, I continued to actively search for a way to play college football. Several colleges sought after me, until I was offered a chance with Gardner Webb College in Boiling Springs, NC and I signed with them. Two weeks before reporting for my freshman year, Coach May, from my high school, called to say that he had taken a job with Livingston University (now known as West Alabama University). Coach May asked me to attend Livingston and play football under him. I liked Coach May, but I had never heard of Livingston University, so I wanted to discuss this with my father. The internet wasn't like it is now, where you can take a virtual tour of the college and find out every detail you could possibly need, and a few you don't. After a very long conversation with my father, I changed my direction, packed up and rode off to Livingston University.

After my first year playing at Livingston, Coach Pete Capo offered me a full scholarship to attend Southeast Louisiana University. My family lived in Rome, GA, which was a four-hour drive from Livingston. Somehow, my father managed to make it to every Livingston University home game. I loved having my dad at my games. In fact, the whole team loved having my dad at the games. He was like the whole team's dad. Southeast Louisiana University just happened to be an eight-hour drive at best. My dad regretfully told me that due to the distance, he couldn't attend any of my games. Well, that is all it took for me. I stayed right where I started and played for Livingston the next three years. There, I was lucky enough to be chosen as President of the Letterman's Club and lettered in football all four years.

After graduating with a major in business and a minor in physical education, I headed back to Rome, GA, for the next chapter of my life. This included marrying my college sweetheart, Cherry Reynolds. We were married for over seventeen years and have two beautiful children, Dr. Cory Mansour and Haley Mansour Hightower. Both are grown and happy in their own successful lives.

Lessons Learned:

- It is important to have a clear goal, whether it is short term or long term. Preferably, you would have both. You should be able to visualize yourself accomplishing your goal. That is how clear it should be.
- There is generally more than one way to accomplish a goal. There will be obstacles in your path, so don't be surprised. Be willing to look at a Plan B, Plan C, or even Plan G, if that is what it takes. Allow yourself to be flexible, but keep your blinders on, staying focused on your goal.
- Respect those around you; work hard and people will step up to help you when you need it.
- Be positive. Think Positive. Stay positive. Surround yourself with people that believe in you. They don't have to agree with everything you say, they just need to have faith in you.
- Trust God. Sometimes your plan isn't His, but He is talking to you and giving you guidance and a better plan. Listen.

Chapter 2

Where My Business Dreams Began

After college, I left Alabama and moved home with my parents in Rome, GA. I had been through four great years of college. I was in full sprint mode to start the next chapter of my life in the real world. Excited that college was behind me, I was ready to go. On my first day home, my mother handed me the daily paper with two job opportunities circled for me to explore. Moms are like that.

So, I headed out into the business world for my first two interviews, one with Frito Lay, and the second with Dalton Health World International, a fitness club.

My first interview was with Frito Lay, where I met with a very professional company associate in a hotel lobby. She told me what the job entailed and explained the benefits package. I am confident in anything I set my mind to and really enjoyed our very direct and to-the-point conversation. I stated I would work very hard for the company. I would load and unload the trucks, drive the route, or even work the assembly line if I had to, but that I was most interested in management.

My second interview was with Dalton Health World International's owner Vick. We met at his health club to tour the facility and I felt very good about the interview. His offer was simple; $100.00 a week and commission-only sales. I told him that I was interested and he said he would call me for a second interview.

I went home to discuss both interviews with my parents. Well, as you can imagine, it was a no-brainer to them. I had a college degree in business and I had a job offer with a good starting salary and a benefits package. "You would be crazy to accept a job at a health club with no benefits. Besides, most clubs close within their first two years," Mom said. My mom has always been a very practical woman. My dad would usually agree with Mom, but I think Dad felt my disappointment. I went back for a second interview with Frito Lay and was offered the job. As I was about to accept, there was a knock on the door. It was my dad and he ask to have a word with me. Daddy Joe said that before I accept the Frito Lay job, I should know that Vick called and offered me the job with Dalton Health World.

Think about it. My dad didn't have to come to tell me about the health club job. He could have let me take the secure job with Frito Lay. I was already adjusting my thoughts to being a Frito Lay manager, but my father knew my heart was into fitness, not snacks. This showed me that my parents were giving me the benefit of the doubt. Maybe deep down they had enough faith in me to believe that I would expand this simple health club job into something bigger. Who knew what that might be…but at least I knew they were willing to watch the ride.

At age 21, I took my first real job, an hour from home in Dalton, GA, working for health club owner and my future mentor, Vick. I shadowed Vick, absorbing every word and studying every detail of the business. A short two months later, Vick told me that he was building a club in Rome, GA, and that I would be transferred to the Rome Sports Connection. I would be working under his best friend at the time, Ted Commander. We presold memberships for six months. Day by day, I was getting stronger, and outselling Ted. After the club opened, it seemed as if I would become the manager, because I was selling well and delegating duties to the rest of the staff. Eight months later, I asked for a meeting with Vick at the Dalton Club and asked to become the manager at Rome Sports Connection. He said that Ted was 35, as was Vick, and here I was

It is NOT Impossible!

a 21-year-old. The truth was, Ted didn't like management. His passion was nutrition, which I told Vick. One week later, Ted became our official nutritional consultant and I was promoted to club manager of the Rome Sports Connection.

The following year, I contacted my college friend, Rocky Beebe, and asked him to come work with me in the organization at Dalton Health World International. Rocky could talk to anyone, and had a face and personality that was unforgettable. For the first year and a half, our team worked six days a week to make the club a success. Saturday evenings we would stretch "starving artists" landscape paintings onto frames. On Sundays, when the club was closed, we would sell them in hotel conference rooms. I bet you can guess what all my family and friends got for Christmas that year.

Being together this much made us just like a family. Vick took me on trips to Las Vegas, Mexico, Chicago, and would spend his holidays with my wife and me. I spent more time with Vick than anyone else in my life, and he was the mentor I always wanted. However, Vick could be difficult on the staff. Out of necessity, I became the liaison for many of the employees and their issues. I'll give you an example. One morning at the Dalton Club, Vick came in early to work out and discovered that the steam and sauna room heaters had been left on all night. It was a payday. He called Rocky into his office and told him because he was the manager on duty, he would be docked for the electricity that was wasted. Vick paid Rocky with four quarters for that week's pay. Rocky was very, very upset and immediately called me. I had to make a stand for Rocky. I told Vick he was wrong, and either he needed to pay Rocky or I would.

One day, out of the blue, Vick told me that he wanted to cover the outdoor pool at the Rome Club. I sold many, many memberships with the expectation that we would be putting a cover over the pool for year-round swimming. As winter approached and nothing was being done about the pool, the members started complaining. I discussed it with Vick numerous times to no avail. I had given my word to these members and it was important to me that we stood by what we told them. His response was that he was not going to cover the pool, and for me not to worry about the members. They would soon forget.

By now, I realized that to work with Vick, you needed to keep your eyes wide open and pay attention. He was a shrewd businessman and not always completely forthright. I never knew what would happen from day to day with Vick, so I really had to stay on my toes. As we commuted back and forth to the clubs, talking about our lives and our futures, I thought we had become close. Vick asked me if I would be with him as a manager forever. I said, to be completely honest, someday I wanted to have a business of my own.

Three months later, when business was going well, Vick approached me with a partnership offer for a new club he wanted to buy in Athens, TN. It was to be named Athens Sports Connection. I was excited at the prospect of becoming Vick's business partner and part-owner of this club, even though he said it needed a full renovation. Now 22-years-old, I was ready for the challenge, and excited to help remodel and open Athens Sports Connection.

Vick explained to me that this deal included the purchase of the land, building, and equipment. It would be sold to us for $100,000. I was asked to invest $25,000 cash to own twenty-five percent of the company, and Vick would front the remainder of the note, which was $75,000. Next Vick promoted me to manager over all three clubs, as well as the four tanning bed locations Vick had purchased. This was an opportunity not to be missed, but I only had $2,000 to my name. I was turned down for a bank loan. My parents offered to put up $17,000, selling an insurance policy to do so. Finally, I maxed out two credit cards to provide Vick with the full $25,000, and, with that, we were officially in business.

I asked Vick about the closing date. Vick asked that I trust him to oversee the loan closing, citing my age as a potential issue. Being new to business and believing my mentor was speaking from experience, I agreed not to attend the closing. A week later Vick gave me a certificate stating that I had twenty-five-percent ownership in Athens Sports Connection. I was very proud. Right then, I began repaying my credit cards and my father, totaling about $500.00 a month. This left me trying to survive on an extremely small budget. The next six months were a whirlwind. I would make the run three to four times a week to four tanning bed locations as well as trips to the clubs in Dalton, Rome, and Athens TN. At that time, Vick began traveling a great deal, and was hardly ever in the clubs. I was making all the decisions, and running the day-to-day operations. When Vick did visit the clubs, it seemed there was always a problem with the employees or the members. In fact, to be frank, the pressure and stress on everybody skyrocketed when Vick was around. One particular day at the Dalton Club, I walked around to inspect the club and found the steam room had not been cleaned or sanitized. I approached one of our team members and asked him to clean and sanitize the steam room. Thirty minutes later, I checked back with our employee and asked if he cleaned and sanitized the steam room. His reply was that Vick told him he didn't have to do it. I marched directly to Vick's office and told him of my concerns. His response was that he was the owner of the clubs and could make any decision he wanted. I was calm, but I came back at him saying that we must have a united front. I couldn't tell the staff one thing and have him come along behind me and tell them something different. He reminded me once again that if I didn't like it, too bad. Realizing that we were not on the same page, I told him that if he really felt that way, I would quit. He quipped back at me with, "You can't quit because you don't have another job and you don't have any money." That was the last day I ever spoke to Vick.

Lessons Learned:

- Look at more than just the practical. Trust your gut.
- People make mistakes. Accidents happen. Make sure the consequences fit the situation.

- Your word is your bond. Tell the truth.
- You know right from wrong! If something feels wrong in your heart, it usually is. Trust yourself.
- Do not undermine others. If you want your associates or employees to respect you, you must respect them.
- Business and friendship are different. Dishonesty has no place in business. Never let another person interpret a contract for you. If you are making a deal of any kind, especially one involving money or property, you must have a contract. Get one and read it yourself. If you need an opinion or interpretation, ask an attorney that is unbiased. If the other party will not agree to a contract, Do Not Do It!
- A contract is not a trust issue. It is a communication issue. It provides clear communication.
- Do not ignore red flags.

Chapter 3

The Ugly Truth Is Revealed!

I arrived home and announced to Cherry and Rocky that I was done with Vick. I planned to sell my part of Athens Sports Connection and start my own business. Since I never received a copy of the closing papers for Athens Sport Connection, Rocky and I went to Athens, TN, to the attorney's office the next day. I asked for a copy of the closing papers. On the way home, I asked Rocky to read the closing papers to me. The biggest shock of my life came next. The papers stated that the land, building, and equipment at Athens Sports Connection on North White Street were purchased for a total of $25,000.00. Rocky couldn't be reading this correctly. I jerked my car over onto the shoulder of the road. I slowly and carefully reread the papers. This was unbelievable. In addition, I discovered that Vick borrowed $75,000 against Athens Sports Connection for new paint, carpet and equipment, AND we were making his payment out of the revenue from the club. This meant Vick's investment was ZERO dollars, yet he owned seventy-five percent of Athens Sports Connection. Wow, this was the deal of the century, FOR VICK. I couldn't believe it! It was hard to contain myself and I felt like tearing him apart. I steamed all night and didn't sleep a wink. I left Rome, GA, at 4:00 am and arrived at Athens Sports Connection around 6:15 am. The club opened at 6:00. I ripped down the club sign in the parking lot and marched inside to alert the members that I was closing the club and to please vacate the premises. Once the members were gone, I locked all the doors. I sat down in the front office, and, for forty-five minutes, answered the phone, informing callers that I was closing the club. Thirty minutes later, three police cars swarmed the building. On site, filling the parking lot, were members and curious folks. This is a very small town where everybody knows everybody. The policemen knew me by name so they knocked on the door to ask me what I was doing, "Closing down my club," I said. I had my certificate of twenty-five-percent ownership in hand. I told them what Vick had done and they figured they should speak to him. Another forty-five minutes went by and they informed me that Vick was on his way. Once Vick arrived, the policeman asked Vick if he wanted to enter the building. He said NO. He thought I was crazy. He asked them to find out what I wanted. I wanted my $25,000.00, and I would leave the premises. He had the police ask if I would take a personal check. My answer was a bank-certified check is all I would accept. Around 9:15 am, Vick arrived with a bank-certified check made out to me. Once the police officer handed me the check, I left to go back to Rome, GA. That was over thirty years ago, and I have not seen or spoken to Vick since.

Lessons learned:

- It is a myth that you cannot work with your family and close friends, but you must choose carefully.
- Never forget where you came from, and who helped you get where you are.
- You can learn every day from others if you keep an open mind. (Although you may not realize it at the time, it will come into focus later.)
- No matter when you work with family, friends, or business associates, always have a contract when making a deal. Remember, a contract is not a trust issue, it is a communication issue. If someone tells you that they do not want to have a contract, this should be a "red flag" for you. Reevaluate your choice of business partners and your entire business decision.

Chapter 4

My Family, My Strength, My Faith and My Passion

IN ORDER TO KNOW ME, you should know a little about my family. They are a vital part of who I am today. Although, along the way, I may not have seen the many lessons I learned from my family. This book has given me the opportunity to look back and clearly identify those lessons.

Daddy Joe (Joe Mansour Jr)

As you have probably noticed, I was very close to my dad. My dad's father died of a heart attack when my father was only four years old. His mother died one year later, making my father an orphan at the age of five. He was raised in Washington, GA, at St Joseph's Catholic Orphanage. He lived there until he was sixteen, then moved in with his oldest sister, Helen, in Atlanta to attend GA Tech. After only a year at Tech, he enlisted in the US Air Force and became a drill sergeant.

My dad was only 5'5" tall, but was one of the biggest men I have ever known. He liked everyone he met and sincerely wanted to know all about them and their family. Daddy Joe's goal in life was to have a loving and close family, and he made sure that is what we became. He taught us how to love others, love God, and give back to our community.

Throughout my father's career in the insurance industry he was Agent of the Year, Sales Manager of the Year, Regional Manager of the Year, and back to Agent of the Year. He was one of those folks who could sell you the clothes off your back and you would be happy that you were buying them. He was genuine. As his company changed owners, merged, and was bought out, the leadership underwent many changes. Dad had a major realization. He really loved the sales process and the people. He hated the firing of an unproductive agent, which is a necessary part of management. He really believed he could teach anyone to be a salesman. The corporate world was more cut and dry, either you have it or you don't…move on. Every year without fail, my dad won all-expenses-paid trips through the success he had in the insurance industry, and he was always asked to do a motivational speech during their sales conventions. He knew his stuff, but he wasn't a corporate-style manager. My father left management and went back to being a sales agent. Although he won Agent of the Year again that year, he was disenchanted with the company and quite unhappy.

By this time, I had already moved to Snellville, Georgia, and opened two Fitness International, Inc., locations, as well as a couple of sister businesses called ProFIT Equipment Center, and The Vitamin Store. After numerous conversations with Mom and Dad, we convinced Dad to leave insurance and come to Snellville to work in ProFIT Equipment Center. I remember the nervousness in his voice about working in the equipment store without any equipment knowledge and experience. But what I really needed from him was a face for the company. Meet, greet, talk, go to community meetings and get to know the people of Snellville. He was a hit. He became the face of the whole organization, a natural PR man. Daddy Joe became the best asset we ever had. Everyone knew Daddy Joe, and he knew every member at Fitness International, and their families.

After working together for many years, Daddy Joe, known as the Miracle Mansour, passed away at the age of sixty-five from colon cancer that had metastasized to the liver. That dreadful day was August 31, 1998. It amazes me that even today, nineteen years later, people tell stories about Daddy Joe and what he meant to them.

I learned from Daddy Joe to stay positive, give to those less fortunate, honor God, treasure family, and to love with all your heart.

My Mother, Ma-Bell (Isabel Marie Deraney Mansour)

Isabel Mansour is one of the strongest women I have ever known, which is good, because she is the backbone of our family. She sees life as black or white, right or wrong, and no horsing around in between. She also taught us to work hard, treat everyone the same, to be true to your word, and to thank God for all your blessings. Sometimes we thought of her as the mean one, because she was the disciplinarian. It is not that Daddy Joe didn't spank us when we needed it, but Mom was the keeper of the rules. Daddy was just one of us boys, and Mama was always one step ahead of us. Once, I did something wrong (I can't even remember what) and Mama was ready to grab me, but I ran. She didn't run after me. She waited. That night, as I was sound asleep in my bed, I was awakened quite suddenly by the pain of a belt whipping me. Mama was on the other end of the belt. I may not remember what I did wrong, but I have always remembered that you don't run from Ma-Bell. Now, she gave a great an example of thinking through a situation and coming up with a plan B…a successful plan B, by the way.

We had a happy childhood. We might of thought that "irregular clothing" was a name brand, but that was fine with us. We had a mom and dad that loved us, which is much more important than an IZOD shirt.

Ma-Bell's family always had clothing stores, so my mother had the merchant business in her blood. At one point when we were young, Mother opened a store called Mansour's Odds and Ends Outlet…and she had everything from footlockers to bolts of fabric to a huge array of women's accessories. She taught each of us the business and had us waiting on customers, making change, going on buying trips, stocking, and cleaning…whatever was necessary. Working alongside her taught me so much about knowing your customer base and real customer service. Thanks to my mom, at 11-years-old, I started thinking about owning a business someday. Even though I was very young I was always thinking ahead. I valued all the lessons my mother taught me. I must also include the influence of my Aunt Helen Richardson. Aunt Helen was my dad's oldest sister, and when we would visit, we would go to her store. She owned a full-service gas station and convenience store before they were popular. She and Uncle Lewis operated that store and I would watch Aunt Helen with extreme interest. I observed everything she did. In fact, she watched *The Tonight Show* with Johnny Carson every night. I thought, when I grew up and had my own business, I needed to watch Johnny Carson, so I would be successful. I do admit, we all seemed to share the bond of entrepreneurship throughout our family.

Fast forward, growing up in the Mansour household, my mom had always been the decision maker. Matter of fact, Mom was the boss throughout my parent's life. I recall six months after Daddy Joe moved to Snellville to work with us (Mama stayed in Rome to sell the house…another lesson in doing whatever it takes), Mom also came to work in the Fitness International corporate office. Both of my parents worked with us at Fitness for ten-plus years. Each year, I would send my parents on a vacation as a perk for dealing with us every day. One of their greatest memories was a trip to the Vatican in Italy. They actually had an audience with the Pope. My dad shimmied his way to the front (it helps to be small) and shook hands with the Pope. My parents were over the moon. They brought all five of us a LARGE FRAMED picture of Daddy Joe shaking hands with the Pope and Mom standing proudly with him. They requested, quite strongly, that we put them in a place of prominence in our homes. And we did.

So, from my mom, I learned to be strong, to stick with my gut beliefs, to do what it takes (which usually means sacrifice), and how to run a business. I also learned that a great woman beside you is priceless for any man.

It is NOT Impossible!

My Sister (AbbieRose Mansour)

(She always said that she had four brothers, and not one of them had to change their name when they got married, so why should she? That's Abbie)

Abbie is the most talented of my siblings. I have always been able to tell her what I'm thinking for my next project and she can help me name the business and solidify the concept. She even helped to design the outside of the Fitness International building. Then she would be off to draw the logo, decorate the facility, write and design all the collateral materials. She would also oversee and create the look of the T-shirts for our many events. I learned to trust her style and decorating even if I couldn't visualize it at first. She'll tell you that there would be much fussing before I would just trust her, but I learned how. Somehow, even on a beer budget, she gave us champagne. She worked on and created the logos, marketing, and interior design for every business I had: Fitness International, Inc., ProFIT Equipment Center, The Vitamin Store, Guaranteed Weight Loss, Collins Hill Athletic Club, Snellville Hall, Fitness Café and even our corporate offices.

Abbie thinks the most like me and has a good business mind. She was a good sounding board because she wouldn't hold back. She supported me, but had no problem telling me what might be a bad idea. Sometimes she was right.

Although she taught water aerobics at Fitness International and did a lot of the design work, much of her career was in pharmaceuticals and testing. She taught Doctors and medical personnel about advanced lipid profiles and cardiovascular testing. She was a good salesman and instructor. I guess she got it honestly.

If you meet my sister, you will never forget her. Like Daddy Joe, she never meets a stranger. Within minutes of meeting someone, she will know their names, birthdays, how they met their spouse, their kid's names and ages, their health problems and hobbies…you see what I mean. Abbie will always introduce herself to the waitresses at restaurants. She will always be the last to leave a function, any function, even church or a funeral. Abbie has three grown children, Dane, AbbiElise, and Brock, all uniquely talented and making their way in this world.

From Abbie, I learned to trust in other's abilities, to see talent, and to expect the best. I have learned that sometimes you can create something from nothing. She reminds me that you can disagree and still love and support each other. Abbie has a belief that people do the best they can at the time, with the information they have. Given the opportunity, they may not do the same thing again. So, give people the benefit of the doubt. Forgive and move on. I recognize that she is the force that connects our extended family and the Lebanese community, and that takes a lot of time and effort.

Paulie, My Oldest Brother, (Paul Joseph Mansour)

Paul was the smart one. He was very intelligent and had an incredibly dry wit. Mom used to say he had a photographic memory. I'm not sure, but he never brought home a book in school and always made A's. At age 19, he enlisted in the US Air Force. While in the Air Force, he earned a bachelor's degree and two masters. He loved to read, hunt, and fly. In fact, he owned two planes, and traveling was his passion. We loved flying with Paul and enjoyed traveling many places together through the years. Paul held many positions in the Air Force, from being the general's secretary, to director of purchasing and requisitions with the civilian offices, to becoming the youngest navigating instructor ever in the Air Force. General Ron Smith recalled that Paul rose quickly through the ranks, and was one of the youngest men to become a Lieutenant Colonel. Paul was 37-years-old. Paul had a teaching spirit. He loved teaching and explaining how things work. He was a leader. On March 14, 1997, at age thirty-eight, Paul and his fiancée, Connie, were tragically killed in his private plane on a flight for a family mystery weekend in Murphy, NC. This was one of the most devastating times for our family.

I learned from Paul that life is short, and that your family and friends need to know that you love them. I saw that you could accomplish great things, even if you were young. I learned there is no disagreement bad enough to stop talking or to hold a grudge. He reminded me that there is always more than one way to approach a situation. I watched Paul take every advantage to teach and share.

Joseph (JoJo), My Younger Brother, (Joseph Mansour III)

Joseph has two traits that make him amazing. Much like my father, Joseph can talk to anyone, and can remember facts about that person after meeting them only once. Joseph has a huge heart and will help anyone, even if it inconveniences him. During high school, Joseph worked at Brownlow Trucking Company, learning the ins and outs of the trucking business from Gene Brownlow, the owner and his mentor. After high school, Joseph attended school and graduated as a certified diesel mechanic. Joseph moved quickly through the business and became an owner/operator of his own tractor-trailer truck. Joseph had two trucks, but his favorite was a big, black and chrome Peterbilt tractor-trailer truck. If there was a spot to dress out in chrome on that truck, it had it. It would stop you in your tracks. She was a beauty. Joseph traveled the US as an owner/operator for ten years.

I remember when we were buying the fitness equipment for our first Fitness International location, Joseph and I drove his big Peterbilt truck to Texas to the Arthur Jones Nautilus equipment warehouse, so we could save over $8,000 in freight. On this particular trip, I met Arthur Jones's son, and he took us on a tour of the warehouse to show us his newest equipment invention. This equipment later emerged as the top-selling fitness equipment in the world called Hammer Strength.

In 1988, Joseph joined me fulltime at Fitness International. He proved to be invaluable. We complemented each other in the business. Joseph has magical hands. He can figure out how to take things apart and fix most anything. He kept all our equipment running. He is self-taught, and had the patience to research and study whatever we needed. He would present me options we could choose from to make a purchase.

He is analytical. I like to cut to the bottom line, and I can be that way because I know that when he researches something, he is thorough and has left no stone unturned. He handled all ordering of supplies for the clubs, and handled the pools and spa equipment. He worked with many vendors. He learned our business inside and out. All the members knew Joseph and loved him. He was one of the main reasons that Fitness International was a growing and successful business.

Now Joseph is a leading agent for Liberty Mutual Insurance. Year after year, Joseph is part of the elite sales club, winning trips, awards, and accolades. I guess he gets that naturally. Joseph has been married to Laura Lynch Mansour for twenty years.

What I learned from Joseph is that you can work very closely and successfully with family. I have learned that you can teach yourself most anything, if you are willing to put in the work. Sometimes, being analytical can save you lots of money. It is smart to have a partner that is not just like you, but has complimentary skills to yours. The best people to have around you are those that are willing to go the extra mile for you.

My Youngest Brother, Michael Patrick Mansour

Michael is much like my mother, and is extremely honest. He lives his life as an example of how he believes people should be. He is black and white and he can love you and disagree with you without putting you down.

In high school, Michael already knew he wanted to be a police officer. He began his law-enforcement career at the Floyd County Police department in Rome, GA. He was there for one and a half years and left to continue schooling at West GA College in Carrollton. While studying, he was hired by the WGC Department of Public Safety as the DUI officer. Michael made a record number of DUI arrests, and in 1985, he became a Carrollton Police Officer. At the Carrollton Police Department, Michael was promoted, and quickly rose to captain. He was selected as the first DARE officer to work in any Carroll County school. He served as the DARE officer for ten years. Like Daddy Joe,

It is NOT Impossible!

Michael loved kids and teaching, so this job was a perfect fit. While working as a DARE officer, Michael was also promoted to Sergeant over the Traffic Division. In 1991, he was promoted to Captain over the Criminal Investigations Division. He served in this capacity until 2004, when he transferred to the Patrol Division as their captain. In 2005, after working for the Carrollton Police Department in many roles over twenty years, Michael became Chief of Police of the Villa Rica Police Department. Chief Mansour is a huge supporter of community policing programs. He is very active in the community and is well loved. Michael is a member of the GA Special Olympics Advisory Board. He is an adjunct professor at the University of West GA. Michael has taught at the University for over thirteen years and covers such topics as domestic violence, criminal investigations, crime prevention, criminal profiling, and gangs. Michael received a BS from West GA College in Sociology in 1986, completed his MPA in police sciences at Columbus State University in 1999. He is a 2000 graduate of the GA Association of Chiefs of Police Command College.

Michael is married to Rebecca Jones Mansour, and they have two lovely children, Gabby, eighteen, who is at UGA in Athens, GA, and Nicholas, fourteen, a saxophone player with the Carrollton High School Band.

Michael had a goal to be in a leadership role in law enforcement. He has shown the many ways that you adjust and move until you reach the top. Michael is all about being a part of a small community and how you can live, teach, and really make a difference. He is a great example of how to keep communities working toward the same goals for the betterment of the city. He reminds me that you can be a leader that is firm but fair, and you will have the respect of those you serve. These are all lessons that I hold dear.

Once again, I do not tell you all about my family so that I can brag that I have great family. Look at your own family. The brothers you played baseball with and wrestled with growing up, and the sister that you had to play dress up with, helped you form who you are today. Maybe this serves as a reminder, observation, or example of behaviors you already knew. Stop and look. Recognize them. Appreciate them. Learn from everyone around you, and you will be better for it.

Chapter 5

A New Day and a New Beginning!

After leaving Vick and Rome Sports Connection, I had no job and no money coming in. Even so, I was more determined than ever to start my own business. At that time, Cherry was working as a real-estate agent but we knew we could only hope and pray for an answer from God. I took the $25,000.00 Vick owed me and paid my father back, paid my credit cards off, and had about $2,000.00 in the bank. I felt I had all the business tools and experience I needed to succeed; the only thing I was lacking was capital.

Rocky called me really upset and fed up with Vick's unprofessional behavior. He told me he was going to quit working for Vick and the health club. I told Rocky to hold on a little longer because I had no job. I couldn't pay him any money and it would be best to give me some time to start a new venture. One month later, Rocky quit. Rocky and his wife, Carola, moved in with us in Rome, GA, and he started working at Kroger.

Rocky, Carola, Cherry, and I lived in a two-bedroom house. Carola was pregnant with their first child, Rocky Jr. We all worked at different jobs. Mine was hitting the pavement every day and trying to make something happen. We all continued to live in Rome, GA. One day, I ran into an old buddy of mine, Ken Smith. He was a member of Rome Sports Connection. Ken and his wife owned a flower shop and worked in the real-estate market in the Rome area. Ken knew I was always actively looking for a place to start my own health club. We both knew it was not a good idea to build a club in Rome, GA, Dalton, GA, or even Athens, TN, since Vick was still there, plus there would be more business competition. One day Ken told me that he had heard a lot about Gwinnett County and said it was the fastest growing county in the US. I drove down to the county seat in Lawrenceville, GA, and looked around the area. I didn't fall in love with the area but decided to visit some businesses nearby. I stopped into a local tire shop in town and was quickly greeted by a man with a huge chew of tobacco in his mouth. He asked if he could help me. I introduced myself and asked if he knew of any fitness centers in the area. He chewed and spit between every sentence, but told me there were a couple in the area (spit). He then said, "Son, if I was you, I would go down there to Snellville. It's a new town and a perfect place to build one of them there fitness centers you are talking about." I sure do wish I could remember his name so I could thank him in person. He was a nice, down-to-earth southern man with a country accent. The kind of man that would make you smile when you met him. I shook his hand and taking his advice, headed to Snellville, GA.

I was in a town I had never heard of, and drove around what seemed-liked forever. The more I drove, the more I began to fall in love with this small hometown community. I discovered there was one fitness center called "The Ladies Club" owned by the Kim brothers.

As I left Snellville and headed back to Rome, GA, I was overwhelmed with all kinds of emotions. I couldn't wait until I got back home to tell my family about Snellville, GA. Sure, I was young, determined, a little naïve, and had no clue what it would take to borrow money, but I was traveling full-steam ahead. I was 22-years-old and moving to a new town where I did not know a soul. I had NO money, NO equity, not a lot of business sense, and I was GOING to build a fitness center from the ground up. Are you laughing yet?

It is NOT Impossible!

Lessons Learned:

- Never judge a book by its cover. The gentleman I spoke with at the tire shop did not appear to be wise, but he gave me some of the best advice I've ever received.
- Keep your family and friends close, because starting your own business can be lonely. There will be lots of times that you will need them near.

Chapter 6

THE BEGINNING OF MY BUSINESS JOURNEY

I STARTED PUTTING TOGETHER A plan of what I wanted to do and where I should start. My first thought was to start talking to some of the banks in Rome, GA, and I visited at least ten different banks within about a three-week period. Per my calculations, I needed a loan for a little under one million dollars to start my business.

To my surprise, I would get the same response wherever I went, "Sorry, son, we cannot do a loan for you." I would smile and each time I would ask, "Why not." A few bank loan officers explained,
1. You don't have a good business plan
2. You have no equity.
3. You are too young.
4. You need a financial breakdown of your business plan.
5. You need area demographics and so on.

Each time I was turned down I would go home and put together whatever that banker said I needed. I counted the times I was turned down for a loan, and within one year and three months, I had been turned down by forty-four banks. It had gotten to the point I wasn't sure which banks I had visited in which city. I had been to banks in Rome, Cartersville, Marietta, Atlanta, Stone Mountain, and Snellville.

Each day, when I would get home, my roommates and wife would ask, "How did it go today? Did anything happen?" I would always have the same answer, "I got some more good information." Sometimes I would come up with some story to keep from disappointing them. One day about six months later, I came home to Rocky and Carola, who were watching TV. Cherry was in the kitchen, and as I said hello to each of them, no one asked about my day. I know they all thought that I was off my rocker and probably never thought I would get the loan I needed. It was a terrible feeling to think everyone had given up on me, but just the opposite happened for me. I pushed even harder. In my mind, quitting was not an option. Seven months into my search for a loan, Cherry and I drove up to another bank in Atlanta. I got out of the car and turned to Cherry to wait for her to go in with me. She motioned that she wanted to wait in the car. The look on her face pretty much told me she thought I was wasting my time. I walked in the bank with my suit on, ready to present my business package. I was trying to look confident and not desperate. I didn't even have $5 in my pocket. Once inside the bank, a tall thin guy, with glasses, dressed in an expensive suit, called my name from across the lobby. He said, "Tim Mansour. Come here, son." As I walked toward his office, I noticed the nametag on his door read, Bank President. My mind and heart started to race and I thought wow, this is it, this is the guy who is going to give me a business loan. With a very stern voice he asked me to sit down, and then closed his door behind us. He came back to his desk, never took a seat, and said to me, "Son, I don't want to embarrass you, but do you understand, as bankers, in the State of Georgia, we all meet at least once every couple of months? We all know who you are, and we all talk about you and your need. I hate to tell you son, but we are kind of laughing at you. So, I am trying not to cause you more embarrassment by telling you that NOBODY is going to give you any money. You are too young. You are asking for a million dollars. You want to move to a town that you have never lived in. You want to open a fitness center, when most of them go out of business within two years, and you don't have any equity. I'm not sure what you are thinking. The only way you would even have a small shot of getting a loan would be from the SBA." As I was listening to him, I began to perk up. I told him that is what I would do. I would get my loan at the SBA. I paused a moment and said, "I hate to ask you, but what is the SBA?" I had no clue what the SBA was, and he began to laugh out loud. He wrote down on a piece of paper, SBA is the Small Business Administration. He gave me the name of a lady, Ms. Kitchens. He told me to go see her, and said, "Please, son, don't go to any more banks asking for a conventional loan, because it's not going to happen".

I headed back home, happy as I could be. Of course, I could not bring myself to tell Cherry about the meeting at the bank. All she needed to know was I had a new lead, and that's all that mattered to me. I contacted the SBA and set up a meeting with Ms. Kitchens. She explained to me about the SBA program, stating that they offer financial help to small businesses or first-time business owners. She told me the SBA did not usually require a lot of money down, but there was a lot of paperwork involved. She gave me a huge package and said exactly what I wanted to hear, "I think the SBA could work for you, but for the money you are asking for, you will need to come up with $108,000.00 in cash and equity." There was only one problem, I did not have anything close to that kind of money. I have the greatest parents anyone could ask for, but no one had that kind of money to risk lending to me.

I went home with a new determination and started searching for ways to get $108,000.00. My friend, Ken Smith offered me $10,000.00, and my sister, Abbie, also let me borrow money against her credit cards. I will never forget going to my first cousins, Albert and Jerry Ashkouti, for a possible loan. I have looked up to these two guys all my life and I think the world of them. I love having them as part of my family. I knew they would have an idea or resource as to how I could come up with more money. I called them and asked if we could meet and discuss my plan. Meeting with them was like being in a very stressful interview. I might be family, but business is business. I explained my plans and the how and where I planned to start. As my descriptions became more vivid, I felt they could actually see the big picture and my dream. I'm not sure if they thought they would ever get their money back, but I will always be grateful for their willingness to support me. They both loaned me $12,500.00, for a total of $25,000.00.

I really started to see my plan was in motion. I was building the money I needed, while pushing, selling, and traveling every day. At one point my parents told me the only way I could make this a reality was to get a business partner. After everything I had been through with Vick, that was NOT an option for me.

My parents and Joseph (my younger brother) owned houses in Rome, GA. Ken Smith (my real-estate buddy) could do appraisals, and we discovered we had around $15,000.00 equity in both homes. God bless all my family; they put their homes in my name, so I could show equity. The pressure was on. I knew I could not fail because I now had all their homes on the line. After getting the equity from the two houses, my father once again offered me some extra money. He had about $15,000.00 and Joseph gave me an extra $10K. By the time, I pooled all the money, I raised the $108,000.00 in cash and equity. This had taken me six months.

My level of excitement was through the roof. I had momentum and was blind to negativity. I was not letting anything or anyone stop me.

My next step was finding land. As I searched, I was turned down several times. One day I found a piece of property designated for a new theater. It was on Wisteria Drive beside Ryan's Steakhouse and Kmart in Snellville. The landowner was Don Barkley. Don was a seasoned businessman who also owned office buildings in Marietta. I paid Mr. Barkley a visit and expressed interest in buying four acres to build a fitness center. He told me he was selling it for $150,000.00, but there was a prospective buyer, a theater. "If they don't want it, I will give you a call." Three weeks later Mr. Barkley called me to say the theater deal fell through. "If you are still interested in the property, I will sell it to you," he said. I was so happy, and wasted no time in scheduling a meeting to talk to him. My brother-in-law, Rod Hokanson, and I went to Mr. Barkley's office to tell him I wanted to purchase the property, and I was going to build my dream fitness center. I'm sure Mr. Barkley had heard this before, but I felt he saw pure passion in my eyes. He could see I was going to do whatever it took to make this happen.

I proceeded to tell Mr. Barkley that I was having a problem. I didn't have all the money to purchase the land, but that I did have $30,000.00 to put down, and I would agree to pay him the rest within one year. He spoke up and said that he usually did not provide financing for property, "And if I do, I charge a high interest rate," so he thought it probably would not be worth it to me. We both paused. Then he said, "Let me think about it and I'll call you back." Three days later he called and asked to meet with me again to discuss financing.

Mr. Barkley was about 60 years old at that time, and I was 22 years old. I made one last push and told him that nothing was going to stand in my way, and I planned to work as hard as I needed. He said he believed I would do well and become successful one day. He wanted me to make him a promise to never forget where I came from. 'There are not many people that I would let borrow money and pay off this loan over time, especially not knowing if I will ever get my money back. I tell you what I'm going to do. You can buy this property, and I'll put it in your name, but I will hold a second note on the property. You pay me $30,000.00 now and I will give you eighteen months to pay the loan off." My emotions almost got the best of me at that moment because I couldn't believe that my dreams were right in front of me and about to come true!

After that meeting, I met with Ms. Kitchens (with the SBA). We met probably twenty times in efforts to push through the loan and get started. I was trying to do everything I could do because I had my whole family's finances and housing resting on my shoulders.

Finally, we sold our home in Rome, GA. Rocky, Carola, Rocky Jr., Paige (she worked with me at Rome Sports Connection), Cherry, and

Tim Mansour

I moved to Snellville, GA, where we rented a home from Paul and Pat Cotter. We all lived in one house. I would say it was a bit cozy.

Now, I had the land and the SBA loan. I had moved my family and friends to a new town and we were raring to go. Everyone had jobs. Rocky and I worked night jobs. Rocky worked at the Golden Gallon in Lilburn, GA. and I worked at the one in Snellville. We would work from 11 pm to 7 am so we could work at our temporary Fitness International, Inc., office during the day. Cherry worked for Jim Hamil at a sign company, and Carola worked at a nursery. Every month we pooled our money to pay the bills.

We lived simply, and we ate a lot of eggs! I remember we would buy food that was out of date, and anything else that was edible and cheap, so we could survive. We did this for about seven months while the club was being built.

Chapter 7

Giving My Dream a Name

We needed a club name. I remember talking to my sister about the name of the club and told her we needed to make the company sound as big and strong as possible. I wanted people to hear the name and immediately think it was a big corporation. I did not want people to know it was owned by a 22- year-old and running on a shoestring budget. I wanted the word fitness to be part of the name, and, thinking even bigger, we started to incorporate the world.

Fitness International, Inc. was born. My sister, Abbie created the logo. We came up with the world globe as the background, and the word FITNESS in big bold letters in front. Abbie then added her creative touch and wrote the word International in her stylized handwriting. It looked remarkable, and a logo was created. This was our first concrete image of my dream, and was just what I wanted.

At the small temporary office in Snellville, we offered FREE aerobics to start building memberships and meeting our new community. This was just one step closer to our new beginning, and making the name Fitness International familiar to the citizens.

Lessons Learned:

- Other people would always tell me that you can't make money without having money. Not true. Look for the opportunity to sell

yourself to the right people. Let others see your vision and allow them to help you. People like to help.
- Don't be embarrassed or afraid to ask questions. If I had not asked what the SBA stood for, I wouldn't have gotten Ms. Kitchen's name. Asking that one important question lead me to my business loan. FINALLY.
- Surround yourself with people that may be smarter than you and willing to tell you the truth and think out of the box. You don't want a board of YES people. They add nothing.
- My motto is, "Do whatever it takes to get the job done, as long as it is morally right." We called it the "<u>Bulldozer Method</u>".
- I started the fire, but I had a lot of great people behind me. We all chose to be positive and motivated. When things got rough, we picked each other up. Surround yourself with good people.
- Everyone will go through tough times. People do well when things are going well. The way to choose people to work with you or advise you is to pay attention to how they handle life when things are going badly.

Chapter 8

THE BIG SEARCH FOR THE GENERAL CONTRACTOR FOR SNELLVILLE CLUB

AFTER MEETING WITH NUMEROUS PEOPLE about plans for our building, I realized most of them wanted me to hire an architect to draw the building plans. This would cost another $15K that I did not have. (Did I mention that I didn't have an extra penny, much less an extra $15,000?) I finally met Russ Sutton with TMC Construction. He was a miracle man for me. He truly believed in me and could see my vision. His company had a CAD machine, and if I agreed to let him build Fitness International, he would personally help me draw the plans on his own time.

After many hours of changing, Abbie putting in her two cents, and redesigning the front of the building, Russ and I completed the final draft. To save money we made a list of items that he could do and a list that I could do to get the job done. My jobs included all the painting, carpet, mirrors, whirlpools, landscaping, and fitness equipment, with the rest being up to him. The building start date was set. After overseeing the start of this process for several weeks, it was tag-team time, and the beginning a lot of manual labor on my part.

Rocky and I, along with Cherry and Carola, would go to the club after work every day. We all pitched in to get the job done! I remember once Rocky and I were painting at the club. We both sat down for a little break and fell fast asleep. I'm not sure of the timeframe, but we were awakened by a man standing over us. He said to me, "Son, it looks like you need help painting. My name is Billy Simonton, and I'm a painter."

I know God sent Billy to help us finish the job. Billy told me that I could pay him when I had the money. I did eventually pay Billy all the money I owed him and he became one of my good friends. Thank you, Billy, may God rest your soul!

During the building phase, I was blessed to meet some really-good people. Many of these people continue to be personal friends of mine to this day, thirty-plus years later. One day in my temporary office, two detectives from the Snellville Police Dept. walked in and began to question me about my business practices. They proceeded to tell me that recently a fitness center in Snellville closed its doors overnight and left owing people a lot of money. They did not want this to happen again. After a few questions of my own, I discovered that they received an anonymous call from someone in Rome, GA, telling them that my intent was to sell memberships, take the money, and never open the club. Of course, there was only one person that was mean enough to make that call and accusation. My initial reaction was not good. I told them that I was there to build a successful business and become an involved member of the community. I had all the proper paperwork to prove my intent. I asked them to leave if they did not have any further questions. One of the detectives was Stan Hall, who I have now known for over thirty years. He continues to be one of my best friends. Much later down the road, Stan married one of my primary employees, Janel Capello Hall.

The temporary office was a great way to meet the community while we were in the building stages of Fitness International. Tracy and Pam Smith were two of the first members to join Fitness International, Inc. Tracy was a wheeler and dealer and talked to everyone. Tracy recruited many members for Fitness International, and he wasn't even an employee. I have conducted many deals with Tracy over the years, and continue to do business with him today. At the time, we first met, Pam was pregnant.

It is NOT Impossible!

She later worked with us in several different positions. Pam is an amazing person. She became one of my most dependable team members, and she worked for several of my companies over the years. I had the pleasure of spending a good deal of time with Tracy and Pam's son, Rocky Smith. We developed many relationships through Fitness International, and were all brought closer as our children grew up together.

Lessons Learned:

- Always be open to meeting new people. New relationships can lead to business opportunities as well as personal growth.
- I quickly learned that the best ambassadors for our businesses were our members!! Word of mouth can make or break your business. A reputation for integrity is priceless.
- When situations arise that are different than your plan, always remember you have options! Think "out of the box" and figure out the best plan for your need.

Chapter 9

It's Here! Grand Opening of Fitness International, Inc., Snellville Club, May, 19, 1986 - What a Great Day!

THE DREAM WAS NOW A solid reality! Fitness International, Inc., was open for business. Our club hours were Monday through Thursday 6 am to 9 pm, Friday 6 am to 8 pm, Saturday 9 am to 4 pm, and Sunday 1 pm to 6 pm. Rocky and I worked every hour, open to close, for one year. We sold memberships, put members on fitness programs, and even cleaned the club ourselves. Our commitment was a glowing testament: "Do whatever it takes to get the job done!" We did!

At that time, my wife, Cherry, coordinated the aerobics program, and Rocky's wife, Carola, managed our children's nursery.

In 1987 the club was doing so well, I placed an ad for a part-time collections job in the local newspaper. Mr. Gene Mark answered our ad. Gene worked full-time as a mortgage broker and part-time for Fitness International as our payment collections person. Gene and I became very close over the next couple of years and spent a lot of time together. With his background, Gene worked with me to help secure financing for different projects. I will always consider Gene and his wife, Angela, part of my family.

Our first club was our baby! I was very particular about the way the club operated, and my front desk personnel were my eyes and ears

Tim Mansour

while I was away. One of my favorite memories in the Snellville Club was of Mr. Bob Forcucci, an early member. One day I walked in the club and began a conversation with our front desk team member. As she was giving me messages and updates, I noticed a lot of food stuffed in the cooler where we kept and sold our power drinks and bars. Almost immediately I began to question her about my discovery, and she said the items belonged to a member at the pool. I quickly reminded her that was against our rules and I would speak directly to the member. I walked to the pool, and upon opening the door, I saw a big stocky guy lying in a chair with crutches in one hand and a cast on one leg and one arm. He looked like he had been to hell and back. I approached him to start a conversation about his food. He quickly smiled at me and introduced himself. I sat down and we talked for a good thirty minutes. I walked away feeling like I had known him all my life. At that time, Bob worked for Snapping Shoals Electric Company as a lineman. On his way home one day, he wrecked his work truck, and had become a member at Fitness International for his rehab. Bob became a part of our fitness family and started working at the club part-time. One of my first memories working with Bob was on whirlpool detail. Ty Ryoul, Kip Rozier, Mike Green, Bob, and myself were digging up our whirlpool that had a leak. About 4:30 am that morning, covered in mud, I looked at Bob and said, "We have too much money and sense to be doing this ourselves." To this day, Bob and I laugh about that memory and the mud from head to toe.

After a successful year under our belt in Snellville, GA, my mind jumped into expansion mode. In looking for a location for our second club, we found another gem, Conyers, GA. During my land search, I worked with realtor Alfred Hewatt, a friend and member. We joined another agent, Charlotte Mercer, in Conyers to close the land purchase. We opened the Conyers Fitness International, Inc., in September 1988.

I started the process that had worked well before and set up a temporary office. This was in a small shopping center beside the building site. When opening the temporary office in Conyers, GA, I was blessed to have my brother Joseph come to work with me. He was very successful himself, as a trucker and diesel mechanic. He gave up his traveling days to help me grow our business. Joseph was the best thing that could have happened to me personally and to Fitness International.

When you are building, the weather is everything. It can help you or hurt you, but it will be part of the building process. Our construction plans for Conyers seemed to be moving along well. The outside block walls were finally up in place, and I was at the temporary office in Conyers when a bad windstorm came rolling through. The storm literally blew the back wall through the building and through the front doors, demolishing our foundation. I was still unaware of what happened when the police rushed into the temp office to inform me of the damage. We walked next door to assess the damage. I remember telling the officers that it could have been worse. He asked, "What do you mean?" I said, "No one was hurt and we have insurance. We have to be grateful for that."

Much later, as the Conyers building was in its finishing phase, I began to look at our business differently. We were about to open a business in a completely different city. While considering the day-to-day operating procedures, we decided to run our business similarly to the McDonald's way. We made the clubs look identical, operate on the same hours, and all the employees would wear certain colors on each day of the week. This gave everyone the sense that no matter which club you joined or visited, everything looked and operated the same. We wanted everyone to be comfortable… It worked.

Here We Grow Again! Fitness International, Inc., Opened Its Second Location in Conyers, GA, in 1988…

We celebrated the grand opening of our second location of Fitness International, Inc., in Conyers, GA, on September 12, 1988.

After the second location opened, it was no longer just about me. We could still operate with a family atmosphere, but we needed the business practices of a corporation. I couldn't be in two places at once. This meant we had to have strong, organized training to develop managers we could trust. We also needed to be able to delegate more. Managing people smarter and keeping everyone on the same page and at a professional level takes practice, skill, and constant communication.

Lessons Learned:

- When devastation happens, you have a choice in how to handle it.
    1. Fall apart and whine about it or
    2. Be thankful (no one was hurt and that we had insurance. I chose to be positive and thankful.) Look for the positive in every situation.
- Always believe in yourself and your dream! Also, choosing the right people for leadership positions is crucial.
- Being the owner of your business does not mean you need to be rude or mistreat your leadership team. Be humble and thankful for every day, no matter what it brings.

Chapter 10

Fitness International, Inc., Snellville location
Bigger & Better!

My life was rapidly growing in more ways than one! My business dreams were expanding and so was my family. At this point, my son, Cory, and my daughter, Haley, were born. My role as a business owner was very important to me but nothing was more important than my children and my role as a father.

It was 1989, and growth within our club was our next focus! With both our Fitness International locations up and running, we realized the expansion of the Snellville location was a must. Due to the popularity of our aerobics program, we decided to build a larger and separate room for our aerobics classes. Our members were outgrowing the club and to better serve them, we felt this expansion was vital. Instead of going with my regular builder for this project, I decided to do business with a member of our club and my church. At the start, we agreed I would pay him with bank draws as each phase of the project was completed. The project was about 75% complete when I started receiving phone calls from the vendors stating they had not received payment for supplies, materials, or labor. I tried numerous times to contact the builder to no avail. I never heard from him again. This mess quickly fell on my shoulders. I discovered he was not bonded, nor did he have insurance on this project. What a horrible mistake it was to use this guy. I called each sub-contractor and set up a meeting to talk them about their payment. I also had four vendors that had not been paid, Poe's HVAC Company, the mirror guy, Ernest Concrete Company, and the steel company. I worked out an agreement to pay each vendor twenty-five cents on the dollar. We all lost money but I felt offering this payment was the right thing to do. A big lesson learned for all of us. Just because someone appears to be honest, acts like a friend, and attends your church, does not mean you can skip checking them out. You must check out a person's credentials and references. Business is business, and you must protect your reputation and finances.

About six months later, I built two more retail spaces onto the Fitness International building, creating a small shopping center. We purchased and owned so much fitness equipment that I decided to open an equipment store. This way I could buy my fitness equipment for the clubs at cost. Previously, I had purchased my equipment from Donnie Floren, who worked for Fitness Depot in Marietta, GA. He knew everything there was to know about fitness equipment. So, I knew if I wanted an equipment store, Donnie was the guy I needed. After many conversations, Donnie accepted a job with me to manage our new retail equipment store. This was a logical, smart investment, because we would be able to purchase all our equipment at cost for the clubs and sell equipment to corporations, schools, and individuals for their homes. We could profit from this type business. Donnie did a great job selling fitness rooms to Georgia Tech, Georgia Power, and several apartment complexes. He also excelled at selling home-use equipment. Our business was called ProFIT Equipment Center, named by my sister, Abbie. She also designed the memorable logo. We held ownership of ProFIT Equipment Center for four years. Then, in 1993, Donnie and his father-in-law purchased the equipment store and moved it to Stone Mountain, GA, renaming it, Fitness Equipment Sales.

When we built the retail space for the equipment store, we also built a second retail space and opened The Vitamin Store. Once again,

It is NOT Impossible!

Abbie came in for the naming and logo design, and I set out to find the best people with the most knowledge for managing and operating this business. I found two perfect ladies, Helen and Ellen. No, they are not twins. These ladies became the "go-to experts" for all our members and customers because they were so well respected in the vitamins/supplements industry. Helen and Ellen managed this store for seven years. The opportunity arose to sell the store, and Mr. Patel purchased the business and remained a tenant for the next ten years.

In additional to ProFIT Equipment Center and the Vitamin Store, we wanted to provide a total experience with the best resources for our members and community. The clubs already had separate rooms for exercise with free weights, circuit machines, cardio, an aerobics floor, a basketball court, track, racquetball courts, separate spas with showers, whirlpools, steam and sauna rooms, a pool, a nursery with a fenced playground, juice bar, tanning rooms, and massage room. We thought we had everything, but looking at the clubs once again, we noticed that members were exercising, but many of them needed help losing weight. Cherry, Pam, and Carola opened and managed The Guaranteed Weight Loss Clinic. Now, we had everything our members needed and were running all businesses in high gear. They must have been pleased. We were voted the Best in Gwinnett by Gwinnett Magazine for seven consecutive years.

Lessons Learned:

- Search until you find the best person for the job.
- Check credentials and know if the company and/or person you plan to work with is bonded and has current insurance. This is important no matter how well you know the person. This is business and it is different than friendship.
- Always ask for referrals, and CHECK THEM OUT. Look at projects they have completed to study the quality of their work. Do your research. This is not a time for shortcuts.

- Even though bad situations may not be your fault, try to resolve the problems, and look at the other point of view. Believe in a win/win resolution. Take the high road and strive to do the right thing!

Chapter 11

FITNESS INTERNATIONAL, INC., EXPANDING AGAIN TO STONE MOUNTAIN, GA, MARCH 1991

WITH PLANS TO EXPAND TO our third location, we were looking for land in a nearby city, Stone Mountain, GA. I met and worked with a real-estate developer in the area named Fred Skebia. The piece of property he had for sale was an out parcel behind a hotel off Hwy 78 that was not visible from the main road. In touring this parcel, I expressed my concerns about the property's visibility. He showed me a set of plans indicating the future development coming to the area. It included two traffic lights on both sides of the cut through, office buildings and apartment living communities. I made a visit to the City Office of Stone Mountain, and everything he had told me appeared to be accurate. I purchased the property at 1925 Glen Club Drive, Stone Mountain, GA. As we were very close to the completion of our building, Fred's other development project fell through and none of the development that was planned ever happened. No lights, no office building, no apartments.

We celebrated our grand opening at Stone Mountain, GA, on March 31, 1991. This was our largest club to date, and was a beautiful 40,000-square-foot fitness facility. It included everything our other clubs had, but even larger, and the pool was an indoor junior Olympic size. This hidden treasure, however, was very hard to find. As many people would agree, location, location, location is the key to great success. This is true. We spent more money on advertising and promotion about where our building was located than all the other clubs together.

The members loved this club and were extremely loyal. We struggled for many months at this location. Still we remained positive that we could overcome the location issue and our club in Stone Mountain would thrive.

Lessons Learned:

- Location, location, location! We learned how important a location is to most businesses. Our Stone Mountain location cost us more in advertising than all the clubs put together. It would have been a wiser plan to spend more money for a location with visibility and easy access.
- Even though we worked hard to duplicate our facilities and our day-to-day operations, every location had its own personality. Know your members/customers, their needs, and community. Be flexible, while maintaining the same level of professionalism.

Chapter 12

LET'S KEEP ROLLING...

THINGS WERE ALWAYS CHANGING. I would tell my staff, "If you are not changing, you are dying," so our motivating motto was "Let's keep rolling." When Donnie moved the equipment store, it left us with a vacant 3,000-square-foot space. In discussing future opportunities with my staff, we wanted to provide a business that could fill in where the community was lacking. In 1993, Snellville Hall event center was created. Abbie came in with a logo and materials and we were open for business.

We would rent out this space for a variety of events. Birthday parties, family reunions, business meetings, church events, and services were the norm. Snellville Hall filled a void for our community and remained open for two years.

As Fitness International was rapidly growing, we discovered our own need for a corporate office. We decided to close Snellville Hall and renovated that space into 18 offices with a large conference room.

The best part of having a corporate office was that I worked side-by-side with my mother and father for ten years. My father was mainly the face of Fitness International. He was also responsible for collecting each club's daily revenue envelopes, doing the bank deposits, and dealing with our member-finance company, First Family Financial Group in Conyers, GA. He also attended all community meetings and Chamber of Commerce meetings. Once, when my parents were on vacation, I was forced to organize all the bank deposits for that week. On each deposit transaction, we had to write a log of all the checks that came in. I came across a check that had my father's name on it, in the amount of $200.00, and I had no clue what he had paid for with this check. After a full day of research, I finally discovered that my father had paid a member's club renewal fees out of his own pocket. Once my parents returned, I sat down with my father and told him he could not pay every member's dues if they did not have the money. He smiled at me and said he knew he couldn't pay for everyone, but that this person was a good member and was going to pay him back ASAP. My father was a trusting and great man!

My honest mother! Her role at the corporate office was as the receptionist. She never missed a day of work and she was never late. In working with my mother, I found out what honesty really meant to her. On numerous occasions when she answered the phone and the call was for me, no matter where I was, (working out, unavailable or even in the men's room) my mother would tell the caller exactly where I was and what I was doing. No matter how embarrassed I might be, she would never waiver from the truth. I spoke to her about any phone calls for me, and asked her not to tell people that I'm in the men's room, working out, or that I don't want to talk to them. She responded, "Why not? That was what you were doing." I smiled at her and went about my business… I have a very literal mother!

Lessons Learned:

- Not all your ideas or decisions will have the ending result that you expect. Do not dwell on what doesn't work. Learn from it and move on.
- Change is not easy but in some cases, change is necessary to grow your business. Always try to look at change from different angles.

Chapter 13

GWINNETT'S MEGA CLUB
FITNESS INTERNATIONAL, INC., GREW INTO ITS FOURTH LOCATION IN LAWRENCEVILLE, GA., SEPTEMBER 1994

EVEN AFTER EIGHT YEARS IN business, financing never got easier! I developed strong business relationships with my bankers. Alan Najjar was one of my main bankers and advisors for securing most of my financing. He sat with me countless times to strategize about securing money for our projects. Alan was one of the main reasons for my success, and I considered him a great and loyal friend. He remains very close with my entire family.

As we looked for financing for Fitness International in Lawrenceville, Alan introduced me to two very important people with Gwinnett Federal Bank, Judy McDaniel and Mickey Wages. Mickey, the Bank President was a lot like us and never took "no" for an answer. As I stated previously, fitness centers are a hard sell to any bank because many of them go out of business within the first two years. I remember one time that Mickey rounded up his board members and brought them in a van to our Lawrenceville property and to visit our other operating clubs. He wanted them to witness how professionally we ran our businesses, as well as to give us an opportunity to meet. I was asking for a $2.3M loan.

Mickey negotiated on my behalf with the board members and didn't stop until they approved a loan of $1.5M, if I could secure another bank to participate and lend me the other $800K.

Mickey told me that the CEO of his bank, Mr. Jim Pack, jokingly said, "I can't believe a man as young as Tim can borrow that much money, and especially for a fitness center of all things." I considered this a huge compliment!

Mickey continued to push hard for me and called numerous banks only to discover most were not interested in lending me any money or participating in our loan. Finally, the President of First National Bank in Lawrenceville, Mr. Glenn White, agreed to meet Mickey and me at his office. We talked business for about thirty minutes and he approved the $800K participation loan on the spot. I could not believe it; this was a great surprise to both Mickey and me. Knowing and getting to the right people is everything in business.

The Building of Our Mega Club, Fitness International in Lawrenceville, GA.

My quest to find our Lawrenceville location was a high priority. After my experience in Stone Mountain, I knew I wanted the club to have easy access and the best visibility possible. I came across two pieces of property on Hwy 316. The one I was most interested in buying was up for sale by Mr. Charles Arnold.

Mr. Arnold was one tough negotiator! At that time, Mr. Arnold had eight separate parcels of land for sale, including the piece I was interested in buying. He was in the position of not needing to sell this property, and that always makes for a very hard negotiation. His starting price was $500K for 2.3 acres. We negotiated back and forth for two or three months. I told him if he would sell me this property, that I believed the foot and car traffic from the club would help sell the other parcels nearby. I felt this was the part of our conversation that sealed the deal. I finally bought the property I wanted for $325K.

No matter how good I felt about this location, there were many people that disagreed. Some people in the area would say the club was going to be too large for that area, and Lawrenceville was not going to be able to support that size facility. They would also tell me that it was too far off the main path on Hwy 316. I would listen to their comments, but I listened more with my gut and relied on the area research I had gathered.

As we started to plan our grand opening, I felt the Lawrenceville club celebration needed to be different. This event needed to impress everyone that walked in the door because it was our super club and it had every amenity you could imagine. We planned a "premier" grand opening with food, drinks and entertainment. We had a professional photographer there to record the event and take personal photos of our guests for the entire evening. We were dressed in tuxedoes to celebrate this special occasion, not the usual party you would imagine at a health club. We invited our entire staff, and all the business leaders that we knew from Gwinnett County and the surrounding areas. I wanted this opening to be a real celebration, showing my appreciation to all who had supported us through the years. Hosting this celebration, the way we did, set us apart from other gyms and gave us the upscale reputation we wanted. It was amazing and the talk of the town.

Fitness International, Inc. Lawrenceville Super Club Opened September 12, 1994

Once the club opened, it seemed like the area around the club exploded. Building started and there was activity around us all the time. From that point forward, the club was always busy. Our memberships were off the charts, and the Lawrenceville club was our best location. The club exceeded every goal and expectation I had.

Grand Opening "Premier" in Lawrenceville, Ga.

Lessons Learned:

- At this point we had over 300 team members. I understood better how to delegate responsibilities. I realized that finding the right people for the right jobs could make you or break you. Promoting team members to the right positions, such as club managers, office managers, assistant managers, etc., and allowing them make decisions, takes constant training and trust.
- Being a manager/owner does not make you a ruler, but should make you a leader.

Chapter 14

Club Business Operations and the Day-to-Day Grind...

Our business operations consisted of running several different businesses at the same time. To maintain operations in the most professional manner, I felt communication for each location was key. We would hold a managers' meeting every Tuesday at 10 am. Every manager was expected to be present and on time. We would discuss any issues that needed to be addressed for each club and our goals for the next week.

My key expectation for each manager was to conduct themselves in a professional manner, dress appropriately, and always be on time. I always stressed to every team member the importance of time management, and would often test them with fun but memorable tasks. One day, I showed up for our managers' meeting wearing my workout clothes. No one seemed to notice. After starting our meeting, I briefly excused myself, only to return wearing a suit and tie. From the moment, I walked back in, everyone began to sit up straight, with all eyes on me, ready to get started. You should dress for success! Give respect and you will get respect. I always made a big deal about being on time because it shows respect and courtesy to the people you are meeting. I would remind them: if you were supposed to meet the president of the United States, how would you dress and would you be late?

We would host quarterly meetings throughout the year. The meetings were usually held on a Sunday afternoon after the clubs closed. I would provide a nursery for those with children, and the meetings were catered so everyone could socialize as a family. Family means everything to me, so we invited our team members' families to join us. This made everyone part of our team. Sometimes there were over 300 people in attendance and we would all break bread together before our meeting.

Chapter 15

Keep Your Eyes Wide Open!

No matter how much you promote a family atmosphere, there will be situations that happen that are out of your control. Some people will steal from you. Others may sabotage your business or want to take control. It could be your management, full or part-time staff, but people will justify their behavior as deserving. Below are a couple of real stories.

One of my top managers started padding our sales books to earn double money on his monthly commission checks. Before we discovered his theft, he had stolen around $9,000.00 within a six-month period. You will find out as an owner that some people that work for you feel like they deserve more than what they receive. Their excuses are; they helped build your business; they work more hours than you or as hard as you do; the business could not run without them; or you just are not paying them enough money. You cannot take these situations personally. This person is a nice guy who has a good heart but saw his personal gain over the company's policy. Most of your employees have never owned a business, and therefore feel that, if you own a business, you are rich and rolling in the dough. Some people that commit a theft are good people, but at certain times can talk themselves into thinking it is right and justified. I have let numerous people go for these reasons and have moved past what happened. It became another lesson for each of us. I learned much more about how people think and rationalize their actions. Since then, we have spoken and amends have been made so that we could forgive and move on. I cannot say that you forget, but I believe I have left these employees with and open communication channel. Many of them still call and visit.

People are human and may become very jealous of you and your family. After being in business for ten years, I had a very disturbing situation happen on a special evening with my family. My family is close, and we always try to make time for each other. Taking turns, once a month, one of us would host a sibling dinner. This was one of those occasions. I was with my brothers and sister at a restaurant in downtown Atlanta when I received an urgent call from two of my managers. They called to tell me they needed to meet with me immediately. I sensed they were upset, but I told them I would meet with them the following day because I was having dinner with my family. They rudely insisted that I meet with them right away, so I agreed to meet them at my corporate office at 11:00 pm that same evening. After finishing dinner with my family, my brother Joseph and I drove directly to the corporate office and sat down with them in our conference room. As the conversation began, we just sat back and listened. They both were very accusatory with their complaints, and said they were tired of the way I would oversee their clubs, and they wanted to make their own decisions. They felt they should not have to go through me for approval for any final decisions. As a manager, decisions should be their business. I remember thinking that they had apparently been scheming and talking to each other about their concerns and seemed to become more and more upset the longer they spoke. They voiced their concerns and anger for about thirty minutes. I asked them if they had anything else to say, they responded no. Since I did not agree with what they wanted from me, I knew there was no saving them or repairing their concerns, so I fired them both on the spot. I asked them to go get their belongings and leave the facility immediately. There was no screaming or yelling from me. I knew they had allowed themselves to be overtaken with dissatisfaction that would travel through the company like a cancerous growth. I couldn't let this happen. Sometimes you must make tough decisions concerning friends or family and do what is best for your company. These two gentlemen had been friends of mine for many years, and this was not a personal decision, but strictly a business one. Years later, we have all spoken and left the bitterness of the situation behind us.

Lessons Learned:

- Some of the tough decisions you will need to make may be against your family or friends that work with you.
- When things don't go your way, try not to make it personal, but try to make a clear and well thought out decision. Be as objective as you possibly can.
- Just because someone does not agree with your ideas, does not mean either of you are wrong. Keep an open mind. Listen and hear what is being said. Sometimes it isn't what is coming out of their mouth, or their actions. Consider everything!
- In the case of a theft or disgruntled employee, it is vital that you become a steady and fair presence in your business. Listen to their concerns. Don't take criticism personally. Remain calm. No one may see the lessons at the time, but allow for the channel to be open, so that later any communication can be welcomed. Believe that people do the best they can in a situation with the information they have. Given another opportunity and more info they may not choose to do the same thing. This is key to be able to forgive and move on.

Chapter 16

THE WORST THREE YEARS OF MY LIFE!

IN 1997 – MY BROTHER, Paul, was tragically killed.

My older brother, Paul, had a brilliant mind and a very strong personality. I shared some very personal issues with him that I wanted to remain between us; I did not want it shared with anyone else. About two weeks after our heart-to-heart conversation, I found out he had shared what I had told him with our parents. I was very hurt. I could not believe he betrayed me this way and I felt I could no longer trust him. In his defense, he felt that my issues and pain needed to be exposed. This happened in January 1996 and we did not speak for almost one year. During this year, we did not talk, visit, or send birthday cards. There was no communication. At that time, we both were very cold and stubborn and rejected any efforts my parents or family would make to help us work things out. On Christmas Day, 1996, our entire family was celebrating the holiday at our parents' house. My brother Paul was there but we never gave each other a single look. As we all were sitting in the living room, I recall making a funny comment about something and Paul began to laugh. This was the first time I had heard his warm, funny laugh in a year. We stared at each other for what seemed to be five minutes. As we stared at each other, it was as if we both knew what the other was thinking and couldn't believe that we had allowed so much time to go by over something so petty. We immediately got up and hugged one another and both broke down in tears. For the next three months, we talked almost every day, hunted deer together, and spent as much time as we could with each other. On March 14, 1997, Paul and his fiancée, Connie, were flying in Paul's private airplane to Murphy, NC, to attend a family *Mystery Weekend*. They never made it to their destination. They were killed in a crash over Joanna Bald Mountain in NC. Our family was devastated! I'm not sure how I could have lived the rest of my life if we had not made up three months earlier. Paul was a very well-known lieutenant colonel in the US Air Force, and for his funeral, General Ron Smith of Dobbins Air Force Base called the White House and asked the president of the United States to approve an Air Force fly over in his honor. He was also honored with a twenty-one-gun salute at his gravesite. I love you Paul and miss you very much! May you rest in peace....

In 1998 – My father, Daddy Joe passed away.

My father, Daddy Joe, loved to exercise. He would come to the club to work out almost every morning before work. Paul's death had taken a toll on my dad and he had lost almost twenty pounds in two months for no apparent reason. He popped into my office one morning after his workout and mentioned he could not button his pants because he was swollen in his lower abdomen. I immediately felt something was not right. My father never drank alcohol and would only smoke a pipe on occasions. He had been a diabetic since age 32, but my mother always made sure he would eat right, and he was religious about taking his medications. Daddy had survived open-heart surgery (a 9-way bypass), and one week after having surgery for colon cancer, he was hosting the Lawrenceville club Premier Grand Opening with us. That is why he was called The Miracle Mansour.

We got him to a doctor right away, and the news was not good. His doctor told us that my dad's colon cancer had metastasized to his liver. He told us that Dad had four large lesions on his liver. We began to discuss his treatments and what we needed to do to help him win this battle. Surgery was not an option, because too much of his liver was compromised. He recommended trying chemo and a lot of prayers. After this discovery, everyone we spoke to told us, with this type of cancer, six months is a normal life expectancy. As every positive family thinks, we vowed to beat his cancer and to do whatever it took to help him live. Four months later, as one big family, we flew to Las Vegas. There were eighteen of us. While we were in Vegas, I remember my father told me he felt better than he had felt in a long time and that he thought he was getting well. This is one family vacation I will never forget. After returning home, my father's health started to go downhill fast. My siblings and I would take turns spending the night with my parents so mother could rest and we could help Dad with anything he needed. My father loved the Braves and would watch the games all the time. One night, while I was sitting with my father, I told him the Atlanta Braves were on TV. He told me he just didn't feel like watching the game that night, and I knew there was not much time left for him. Two weeks later, we placed my father in hospice. He passed away August 31, 1998. To this day, Daddy Joe's service remains the largest funeral held at our church, St. Oliver's Catholic Church in Snellville, GA. He is the only person from our church parish that has a statue of St Joseph on display in his honor.

In 1999 – My Divorce

After seventeen years of marriage, and two beautiful children, Cherry and I decided to divorce. This was a very dark and unhappy time that constantly made me feel as if I had failed. She is the mother of my children and I will always feel very blessed and connected to her through our children. She is a great mother. Many years have passed and I can thankfully say we are very close friends. We share in the responsibilities and decisions in our children's lives, and celebrate their accomplishments and birthdays together. Today, she is our realtor and continues to work with us on a weekly basis.

Chapter 17

Holding a Grudge OR Letting It Go!

Grudges destroy people! The longer I have been in business the more I notice how many people hold a grudge against someone in their family, an old friend, or a work associate. As time passes most people can't even remember what the grudge was about. From my own experience with holding a grudge, I have learned it only destroys you. The thing most people don't understand is that it does not hurt the person they are holding the grudge against. Instead, it stores hatred in your own heart.

My grudge with Paul lasted for eleven and a half months. I thought I was being tough but realized this only made me weak. I lost one year of time with him because of this foolish act. We repaired our relationship only three months before he died. I made a vow, to my family and to myself, that I would never hold a grudge again. For the last eighteen years, I can honestly say that I have not held a grudge toward anyone. This does not mean you need to become best friends, go into business with someone, or even spend time with them. Vowing to not hold a grudge will help you keep from holding negative feelings, resentment and hatred in your own heart. It's exhausting!

Let me ask you, do you have a grudge against someone? If you do, is it worth holding hatred in your heart for them? This is something to consider because "what if" they died, they got cancer, or if something happened to their family? Could you ever forgive yourself? I couldn't.

God gave me a second chance and I learned my lesson. I hope you don't have to learn this lesson the hard way.

My challenge to you is live your life without grudges! In business, family, and friendships, there will be plenty of aggravation and sometimes people will hurt you. Life happens. I am not saying you must forget the grievance. I hope you will learn from it. Not everyone you meet will like you or agree with you. Just believe in agreeing to disagree and release it.

Lessons Learned:

- I learned that holding grudges hurts you more than it hurts the person you are holding it against.
- Grudges put more stress in your life, affect your energy, and will drain you emotionally. Try to resolve any grudges you are holding in your life. Focus your energy on something worthwhile. You will be much happier.
- My quote: "Work hard at forgiving others, not only for the other person's sake, but because you deserve peace."

Chapter 18

TENNIS, ANYONE?
COLLINS HILL ATHLETIC CLUB (TENNIS FACILITY)
PURCHASED IN NOVEMBER 1999

AT FITNESS INTERNATIONAL IN LAWRENCEVILLE, GA, a guy named Dennis (a tennis pro) worked in our Pro Shop. One day, he asked me to go with him to look at a facility he was interested in buying and give him my opinion. I eagerly accepted, because I love looking at new business ventures. The facility he wanted me to look at was only 1.25 miles from our Fitness International Lawrenceville location. It was a tennis facility called Countryside Tennis Center. We noticed it was a nice building, and there were sixteen courts. As we were touring the building, it had a cold and empty feeling. However, I could see that it held great potential with some attention and the right person in charge. Once we left, I shared with Dennis the building improvements I felt would be necessary. Adding a large outdoor deck for entertainment that would allow people to watch tennis matches, adding a full bar and grill area inside, adding an exercise room with aerobics to help bring in more members, and making it a member-only facility were some of the changes I felt were immediately needed. Two weeks later, Dennis let me know he could not secure financing for the $1.2 million-dollar purchase. A few days went by and I mentioned to Dennis that I would like to look at the building and property again for myself, if he didn't mind. I revisited the tennis club, because, somehow, I knew it could be a prosperous business. Before every business venture, I visualize walking through the facility and seeing the finished product. The following week I met with the owner of the tennis club, Bill Thornton, and he told me he was asking $1.2M. I expressed interest in the club and told him I would only pay $750,000.00. I knew the facility had not made money in the ten years that it had been in business and I would have to invest a large amount of money to upgrade the building, courts, and grounds. Bill told me "You are crazy as hell, and I will never sell this club for that price." I said no problem, and walked away. One month later, I was at our corporate office in Snellville, GA, and Bill called, I answered the phone, and someone said to me, "Is this Tim," I replied yes. The caller said, "Does that offer still stand?" I was somewhat stunned and did not recognize the caller or what he was talking about. I finally realized it was Mr. Thornton from the tennis club, and he was ready to negotiate. He agreed to sell me his business for $750K but he wanted to keep his lawnmower. I told him I didn't even know there was a lawnmower there, and made the deal with him over the phone.

I knew it was going to be tough to get the financing because the business wasn't profitable and needed a lot of improvements. I also knew I would have to find a banker that I had done business with before. The banker had to believe in me and see my vision for the place, so I met with Judy McDaniel from Gwinnett Federal Bank. We walked through the tennis club, and I remember Judy telling me she would not lend money for this facility to anyone else but me. She said she had seen what I had done before in business and knew I would make it successful. Thank you, Judy. What a great compliment!

We bought and closed Countryside Tennis Center in November 1999. Once the business loan was approved, it occurred to me that I did not know anything about the tennis business. I started asking around, and was given the name of a guy who had been in the industry for many years, Mr. Aubrey Jackson. At that time, Aubrey worked at Four

It is NOT Impossible!

Seasons Tennis Center. I decided to visit Four Seasons to meet Aubrey and hopefully talk to him about the business. After talking to Aubrey for a while, I asked him if he would mind sitting down with me again so we could talk about the tennis business and I offered to pay him for his time. Aubrey was very well known in the tennis world and local community. If anyone knew tennis and how to coach teams, individuals, and even kids, it was Aubrey. Within a few days, we met again over coffee, and Aubrey told me that he had enough and was getting out of the tennis business. After hours of sharing the great potential that I thought the tennis club had, I asked Aubrey if he would reconsider staying in the business. He could come work with me to make our tennis club successful. After much consideration, Aubrey took the job as our tennis club manager in January 2000. Aubrey immediately went to work on building programs, organizing teams, and interviewing our tennis staff. Because Aubrey had been in the tennis business so long, he would be able to tell me the best tennis pros to help us with certain programs. We hired a well-known tennis pro in Atlanta, Dave Matthews. Dave had a big kids academy and came to work for us in January 2000. Aubrey and Dave worked side by side with me through all the club renovations. Abbie did the logo and the interior design work and we were ready for a Grand Opening. With a newly renovated facility, we reopened in March 2000 as Collins Hill Athletic Club.

The club became very successful quickly, and was for many years! We had adult and kid's programs, a large-number of tennis teams, camps, swimming, kid's academy, junior tennis tournaments, and we were the first tennis club in our area to host two 50K Pro Tennis Tournaments.

Chapter 19

CREATIVE MONEY MANAGEMENT

THROUGHOUT MY 30 YEARS IN multiple businesses, I have borrowed money in more ways than I can remember. During the years, I have been in business, we have enjoyed many financially successful years. However, I would be remiss if I didn't mention that we had some very, very tough years as well. When you own your own business and you are the only one finding money, you must learn to become resourceful in many ways. I have borrowed money many different times, from my family, friends, and whomever would lend me money. No matter how much I owed, regardless of the stipulations, I would always find a way to repay my lenders.

Once I went to SunTrust Bank with my mother, because she was going to lend me $30,000.00. As she handed me the money, she paused, looked me directly in my eyes and told me, "This was the last time I can lend you money, because I am just too old to do this anymore." I'm sure it was stressful for my parents to lend me money and I'm sure they prayed often that I would get it back to them. I remember overhearing several of my family members saying to each other, "Make sure if you have any extra money, you do not tell Tim, because he will be asking you for a loan very soon." Even I had to laugh.

The payment for all four clubs was $52,000.00 a month. The power bills were around $15,000.00 p/m, and my payroll was right at $43,000.00 p/m, counting other monthly expenses, our monthly payables would total around $150,000.00. At times our receivables for the month would vary from $130,000.00 to $170,000.00 p/m. It doesn't take a rocket scientist to understand that experiencing a couple of bad months would easily throw you into the red.

Over 30 years we were in the red more times than I care to admit. Being in business for yourself, and what many business owners understand is, you have one of two options, SINK OR SWIM! I was determined to swim for my life. I became a great swimmer because I had lots and lots of practice.

The hardest thing to do is borrow money when you absolutely have to have it. I borrowed money from my brother Joseph on numerous occasions. The last time I approached him to borrow money from him and his beautiful wife, Laura, I needed $200K. All I could see was fear in their eyes. They are two of the hardest-working, most-conservative people I know. I felt very embarrassed and sorry for them, but I did not have a choice. I always paid them back. I thank God for all the chances they took on me and for believing in me.

I have so many stressful financial memories, but one time that stands out in my mind was when I was two-and-a-half months behind on the club mortgage payments.

I decided to go on a short weekend trip to clear my mind. Thursday morning, I headed out of town. The following morning, I received a frantic call from my brother, Joseph, telling me that NationsBank had placed a foreclosure notice for the clubs in the newspaper. I returned home that afternoon to deal with this catastrophe.

At this time, we had over 20,000 members total for all four locations. I knew this news would be devastating to our business once the members read the newspaper. My next decision did not have a black and white answer. Friday evening I called the newspaper to tell them the bank had made an error on their post. I wrote a letter to our members to reassure them that our club was in good standing and ask the newspaper to print my letter on Monday morning. It was my desperate hope that the out of state bank would not see my letter, because I needed time to plan a strategy to keep the business afloat and our doors open.

I spoke to the NationsBank on Monday morning and they required me to make two payments in the amount of $104,000.00, plus late fees, or they would continue foreclosure proceedings. I pulled $40K plus from my credit cards, but this did not satisfy NationsBank.

NationsBank informed me they would continue foreclosure proceedings and gave me forty-five days to refinance the $5.2M loan for all four Fitness International locations. I called everyone I knew to try and figure out a way to get this money. I finally talked to a high-risk financial institution, Amresco Finance, in Boise, Idaho. After many phone calls, they flew down to see our facilities and finally agreed to give me the $5.2M loan to refinance all the clubs. The loan they offered was very high interest with the stipulation of enhancement fees. My loan was included with five other businesses. The way this worked was when another company in your pool of money falls behind on their loan or goes out of business the other businesses must pay their part calculated on the percentage they borrowed for the pool of funds. Three businesses went out of business and I paid $4,700.00 extra a month on top of my monthly payment for 24 months. The loan I received from Amresco Finance was closed on August 31, 1998, the day my father passed away. NationsBank showed me how much they cared about their business relationships.

These stories represent just a few obstacles we faced in our thirty years in business, and are the true and brutal facts of my journey. I wish I could tell you that going into business for yourself will not be an everyday battle. I would never take back my business experiences with my family, friends, and colleagues. These experiences taught me lessons that will remain with me always. During the tough times, I remained hopeful and positive. I can honestly say that ninety-five percent of my family and friends never knew these struggles were happening.

Lessons Learned:

- All my life, people have told me that whatever I touch turns to gold. You may think this about other people around you, but I can assure you that no one before me or after me has a perfect life. There will be challenging situations in everyone's life. It may be sickness, money problems, or the death of someone close to you. It's not if it's going to happen, but WHEN it happens, HOW will you handle it?
- A person will show you their true colors not when things are going well, but when things are going badly.
- Treat people with honor and respect and most of the time they will have your best interest at heart.
- Creative, out-of-the-box thinking is a must in business. Train yourself to see beyond what is in front of you.

Chapter 20

How to Weather the Storms of Your Business!

Business has its harsh realities! If you have ever been in business for yourself, you will understand, like anything else, there will be good and bad. In good times, everyone is happy and thriving. In bad times, you will be tested in every direction. Remember, it's how you handle the bad times that count. The bad times can make you or break you, and can have you hanging up a GOING OUT OF BUSINESS sign before you know it.

I have worked very hard at making sure our team members were well informed and trained in all aspects of business relations. We held monthly meetings that we would video tape for our current-team-member and new-hire employee training sessions. These refresher and training videos would address topics such as expectations for cleaning the facility, sexual harassment trainings, sales training, front-desk courtesies, CPR training, to our current or updated human resource info.

In business, especially with 300-plus employees as well as 1000's of members, you will have lawsuits. At Fitness International, we experienced our share of frivolous lawsuits. This includes everything from a member who tried to work out with too much weight, lost his balance, and ran into a mirror; another member that fell off a step in an aerobics class and a member on her way out of the club, tripped on the carpet, fell and hurt her knee. These lawsuits never had merit, and all it cost the company was a letter from our attorney to have these claims dropped. One case, that was settled by our insurance company, was with a member that claimed, when getting out of the shower at the club, he slipped and fell. Even though we had slip-resistant tile installed, our insurance company felt it was best to pay $7,000.00 to settle this claim and not go to court. A female employee that had not worked for Fitness International for over two years filed a criminal lawsuit against one of our previous managers, who had already left our company. She was suing him for sexual harassment. She was unable to collect money from this lawsuit. Two weeks before the statute of limitations ran out, she filed another lawsuit against Fitness International, and me, personally, with the claim that I never trained our employees in the correct manner to avoid or prevent sexual harassment. She sued us on seven different counts for a total $2.5M. Our attorneys investigated all counts against Fitness International and me and felt her accusations were unfounded. My attorneys called the other attorney to state our position, and the other attorney requested that we settle for a lesser amount of $1.6M. We refused and said we would be requesting a jury trial. We knew we were going to court, and our insurance would not pay out any money, since we had no coverage for sexual harassment claims. Our trial lasted for a grueling two weeks. We had over fifteen witnesses that testified on our behalf. Some of these people had already left the company, moved out of state, and a couple had been previously fired, but they all said they liked working at Fitness International and were treated fairly. They testified that as employees of FI, they were trained with a zero-tolerance policy against sexual harassment. As the plaintiff took the stand in court, she continually changed her story about her claims against the manager and the actual events. We felt very strongly that the jury did not believe her story. At the end of the trial, all seven counts against us were dropped with no compensation to the plaintiff. Even though Fitness International and I were found one-hundred-percent innocent by the courts, it still cost us $125,000.00 in attorney's fees to defend ourselves from these claims.

It is NOT Impossible!

Lessons Learned:

- Continuously train employees on the newest laws concerning sexual harassment.
- Take all accusations seriously, and try to handle the situation before it goes to court. You never know how it will turn out when facing a jury.
- Have property insurance in place to handle any catastrophic situations (accidents, sexual harassments, etc.) that may arise.

Chapter 21

THE DECISION TO START SCALING BACK THE BUSINESS!

IN 2001, WE SOLD OUR Fitness International, Stone Mountain location. As we started to look at our company as a whole, we knew that one of our clubs was not producing a positive cash flow. After ten years of struggling with the Stone Mountain location, and spending more money for advertising than all our clubs put together, we made the decision to cut our losses and sell. We owed $1.2M on our Stone Mountain club and sold the club for $850K. We estimated that we had lost over $800K in our ten years in business at this location. Even though we managed this club exactly like the others, it did not thrive the way we would have liked. Tough times are about how you handle it!

In 2002, Gold's Gym of Conyers, GA, wanted to purchase our Conyers club. After months of negotiations, we sold our Fitness International Conyers location for $1.3M.

In 2003 we received an offer from one of our previous managers and a good friend, Ty Ryoul, and his associates Chuck and Bridgette Morris, owners of Snellville Glass Company, to purchase our Fitness International Snellville location for $1.4M. After purchasing this location, Ty managed the day-to-day operations for seven years, and was very successful.

At this point, our focus was on our two Lawrenceville businesses, the Fitness International Super Club and Collins Hill Athletic Club.

Lessons Learned:

- Bigger is not always better. You want to make sure each facility is thriving independently and your books are in the black most of the year.
- You need to learn when to grow/expand, and when to cut back or sell.

Chapter 22

The Best Part of My Life, My Children and My Wife!

My Children: Cory Mansour, MD and Haley Mansour Hightower

The days that my children were born were the proudest days of my life. Becoming a father has truly enriched my life.

Cory was the first grandchild in the Mansour clan. He is a natural athlete and could have played baseball or tennis for most any Division-1 college, but since he was fourteen, he knew that he wanted to become a doctor. Cory reminds me of my brother, Paul. Like Paul, he is a brilliant and focused young man. Cory graduated from University of Georgia (UGA), in May 2009 and continued to the Medical College of Georgia in Augusta where he graduated in December 2013. Cory is now a doctor of Anesthesiology, currently in the process of completing his residency. In March 2012, Cory married his high school sweetheart, Lauren Wilbourn Mansour. Lauren also graduated from University of Georgia undergrad, then graduated from UGA law school in May 2012. She passed the Georgia Bar and South Carolina Bar, with flying colors. Lauren is practicing with an established, successful firm in Georgia. She is an amazing person and very special daughter-in-law.

Haley is my only daughter, and is, in many ways, just like my mother. She is strong and determined. If she has an opinion, you are likely to hear it. She sees in black and white, right and wrong, without any grey. Haley is honest. She really cannot tell a lie. I love that about her. Haley graduated from Grayson High School in 2009. Being a real animal lover led her to study animal care and grooming. Haley married Terry Hightower in April of 2014 and resides in Winder, GA. They both currently have successful careers at Kubota Manufacturing.

The lessons I have learned from my children remind me every day to thank God for my blessings. Cory and Lauren are excellent examples of focus, doing what it takes to achieve a goal and not allowing circumstances to knock you off course. They remind me that sacrifice now has great rewards for later. Haley has taught me to accept people for who they are and to see the good that they offer in the world. People are different, but everyone can play a part in being an asset to society.

The Day I Married the Love of My Life!

Before ever knowing Chrystal, I knew her father, Mr. Jewitt Williams. Mr. Williams worked with me at our clubs as my painter for more than 15 years, and this is how I met his daughter. Chrystal worked full-time in the banking industry, and in 1988, joined Fitness International, as a group-fitness instructor and part-time evening front-desk receptionist. She was with us in this capacity for nearly 8 years. After that, Chrystal continued working in the banking industry for 22 years while following her group-fitness instructor passion and training on her own.

Mr. Williams died in April 2000. I reconnected with Chrystal and we started dating. We were married in May 2003.

My Wife, Chrystal Williams Mansour

It is easy to describe my wife. She is beautiful inside and out, has a big heart, is caring, loving, vivacious, and strong as a rock. Although she is only 4'11", she stands tall and accomplished in all that she does. Chrystal is my gift, directly from God, made just for me. Just as Daddy Joe had my mother, I have my loyal Chrystal. From the first day, I met her, she has been there to support me during the good, the bad, and the ugly times of my life. I love being around her and am honored to be her husband. She makes me a better person and she is the sunshine of my life. (I think there is a song like that.) Chrystal may stand beside me in support, but she is in the forefront of her own accomplishments. She has 22 years of banking experience and has been a group-fitness instructor for 30-plus years. She is unarguably one of the best group-fitness instructors in the industry. She attributes her success to her determination and dedication in helping others achieve a healthier lifestyle. Chrystal is genuine. Like Daddy Joe, her birthday is May 28, and she is a real people person. Chrystal has been by my side in our business ventures and takes it upon herself to study, research, and learn whatever is necessary to help us be successful. She is smart, disciplined, focused, self-taught, and fearless. She can be in shorts digging in the dirt one minute and the next minute, on my arm, attending a gala dressed in an elegant gown. Chrystal and I are complementary to each other, in that she is the analytical one and I am the cut-to-the-chase guy. I stand behind her with pride, and support her in her endeavors, as she does in mine. I feel as though our world is a better place because of Chrystal and I am truly blessed. I cannot imagine my life without her!

I learn things every day from Chrystal, like how important it is to stop and talk to people, listening with interest. She reminds me to be fiercely loyal. She shows me patience. She has a heart that serves others and gives to those around her that are less fortunate. She has taught me to experience love fully.

Chrystal is the love of my life! She is a very hard working person and has an enormous heart. Chrystal started working full-time at Fitness International in 2003. She helped me with accounts receivables and taught aerobic classes. She eventually managed The Party and Event Center at Collins Hill Athletic Club, as well as our front office.

My children love Chrystal very much, and she loves them with all her heart. I will always appreciate and treasure her for all the love she has given to us. Chrystal has been my right hand for many years. She has also been through some of the most stressful times in our business and in my life. I recall a very surreal moment after Chrystal and I were married. The vows, for better or worse, were tested and without pause; she leveraged her home to help us survive one of those financially tough times. I also remember her receiving a $90,000.00 inheritance from her family, and with no hesitation, giving it to me. Chrystal is someone I can always count on, no matter what, and continues to support me in all our endeavors.

Chrystal and my ex-wife, Cherry, have been through a lot over the years, and are now great supporters of each other. I don't think I have ever said it out loud, but I would like to thank Cherry for her forgiving, kind spirit and being a part of our life. Divorce is never easy, and I can personally attest to that fact. It takes a tremendous amount of work, maturity, forgiveness, patience, faith, prayers, and strength to move your life onto a new path. Cherry is happily remarried and knows she will always be part of our family. Realizing we will always be connected through our children and the support of family has made our life changes a success. My kids are happy and life is great. I will never forget my life with Cherry, and I will always wish her nothing but happiness.

It is NOT Impossible!

The Mansour Family

Chapter 23

THE NEGOTIATION OF MY LIFE WITH GEORGIA GWINNETT COLLEGE

IN 2004, AFTER SELLING MOST of our businesses, we were left with the Fitness International, Lawrenceville, GA, location and our tennis club, Collins Hill Athletic Club. We worked very hard for the next two years running these two businesses, and I was looking for ways to improve our foot traffic in the clubs. In 2006, the first four-year college in 100 years came to Gwinnett County and was being erected right beside our Fitness International super club on Hwy 316. The name of the college is Georgia Gwinnett College (GGC), and, at that time, Dr. Daniel Kauffman was its president.

Also at that time, my son, Cory was a freshman at the University of Georgia. Looking at his first semester bill, I noticed he was being charged a fee for the college's fitness center. I asked Cory about this charge, and he told me he did not have time to visit the fitness center, but that every student was charged an amenity fee. Wow, the light bulb lit up! My thought was I wanted to set up a meeting with Dr. Kauffman and express interest in applying the same structure with our two facilities, GGC and Fitness International.

I knew Dr. Kauffman was an avid exerciser, so I felt very comfortable going to meet him to discuss my plan. I also knew Dr. Kauffman was a Brigadier General in the US Army, and since my brother was a Lt.

Colonel in the US Air Force, we had much in common. We hit it off from the start. At the time, I met with Dr. Kauffman, the student enrollment for GGC was around 118. He said his goal was to grow the enrollment to over 10,000 students within the first five-years. In my presentation, I laid out what I thought was a win/win approach for both of us.

My plan suggested that every student enrolled at GGC would automatically become a member at Fitness International. Each student's tuition would include a $50.00 charge per semester, for full access to FI and its programs. Once the college collected their fees, GGC would pay 50% of the total amount collected to Fitness International. I felt this would be a good plan, because we would both make good money without any out-of-pocket expenses. The students would have access to a 52,000-square-foot fitness complex for only $16.00 a month. I further explained that any interested faculty member would also be eligible at the same low rate. As I was leaving, Dr. Kauffman stated he was very interested and would be in touch after he could present this plan to the board.

Two weeks later, the vice president of the GGC, Eddie Beauchamp, came by to meet with me. He said Dr. Kauffman liked my offer but expressed more interest in purchasing our facility, land, and building. I told Eddie I would be interested in discussing this new option. He asked how much money I was asking to sell them all of Fitness International. I told him I would be back in touch with him in a few days. I began my due diligence and had an appraisal done. I called Eddie with my asking price of $6.0M for land, building and equipment. One month passed and Eddie called me, he said they had talked to the college, and they were more comfortable paying $4M. Over the next 1 ½ years, the college and I negotiated back and forth. I finally told them my bottom-dollar price was $5.5M. Things began to change rapidly! With the 2007/2008 economy crash, we were losing members daily. Also, before the deal had been completed, our members heard outside rumors that GGC was purchasing our club, and was not going to allow anyone but the students to be members. These rumors affected my financial

It is NOT Impossible!

bottom line tremendously and in a very short period, I was behind three months on my mortgage payments for a total of $75,000.00, plus late fees. I was smack in the middle of a balancing act. I was dealing with my bank, Amresco Finance, because I was behind on my payments and did not want them to start foreclosure proceedings. I was also dealing with the college, trying to show a strong front for negotiating power. I knew if Amresco started foreclosing on FI there was a chance they would list the club in the paper. Once this happened, I knew my asking price would go down drastically. I contacted Amresco and told them I had a buyer for the club and asked them to give me a discount on my loan. I told them if they would work with me I would pay the discounted loan amount in full. I knew Amresco had two options, they could foreclose on FI and sell the building themselves, which I knew they did not want to do, OR they could take a chance and give me a little more time to pay off the loan. Amresco called me back and asked me how much of a discount I was looking for, and who was my buyer? I knew I could not let Amresco know who was interested in buying the facility, nor could I let the college know my situation with the bank. Of course, the reason for this was I was in the middle. Both parties could have made a better deal without me. I called Amresco back and told them I could not disclose the buyer, but I was asking for a $500,000.00 discount, and wanted them to also knock off the $75,000.00 I was behind, plus late fees. I also told them that I did not want the $575,000.00 discount to show as income back to my business. One week later, Amresco called me back and said they were willing to take the debt I owed which was $2.3M and reduce it to $1.8M, they would subtract $75,000.00 and late fees, but my loan needed to be paid and closed within forty-five days, or they would accelerate the foreclosure proceedings. During these negotiations with Amresco, I would regularly confide in one of my good friends, and banker, Alan Najjar. I told Alan about this deal, and that I had asked Amresco to send me a letter outlining their offer. He told me there was no way Amresco would agree to this and if they did it would be a miracle. Two weeks later I received this **miracle letter** from Amresco! Ask for what you need. You will never know if you don't ask.

Negotiation is power, and sometimes you need to listen to your gut! Around a week later, Eddie from the college called me to ask me to meet with him because he thought we had a deal. My brother Joseph and I were excited beyond belief and went to meet Eddie at his office. We walked in his office and he began the conversation by telling me the college had looked at the entire deal and they were happy to offer me $4.2M. My heart sunk and I became very upset. I looked at Eddie and told him, he had wasted a year and a half of my time, and the college apparently did not want this deal. I turned and left his office. I recall the conversation my brother Joseph and I had on the way back to the club. Joseph was really upset with me and could not believe that I walked away from this deal. He reminded me we could lose everything, and Amresco could foreclose on us, take our building, and leave us with nothing. I am not sure why I felt the way I did, but I told Joseph that I didn't think it was over, because Eddie never told me the $4.2M was their final offer. I went back to my office and twenty minutes later, Eddie called and asked me to come back to his office, he was ready to finalize our deal of $5.5M. I went back, made the deal, and felt that the weight of the world had just been lifted off my shoulders. Some chances are worth taking, and the good Lord blessed me with the ability to negotiate the deal of my life! About two weeks later, I received a deposit into my account for $5.5M. When that money hit our account, we all literally cried with joy. I immediately paid off all my debt and was ready to focus on what the future held for my family and me.

On January 31, 2008, we closed the last location of Fitness International, Inc. We transferred over 4000 members to Lifetime Fitness. Our agreement with Lifetime stated that they would honor all the membership rates our members were paying for the duration of their contracts. Our Fitness International members were happy, my family was happy, and I was happy. My wife Chrystal and I took some much-

It is NOT Impossible!

needed time off. We purchased our home, and worked on its renovation for six months, before eventually setting up offices at our tennis center to help run the day-to-day operations of Collins Hill Athletic Center.

Lessons Learned:

- When negotiating a deal, don't be too nervous to take a chance; just be sure you can live with the end-result whatever it may be.
- Remember a deal usually doesn't happen when it is only good for one side.
- You cannot build a successful business by yourself. Always take care of your employees and the people that helped you become successful.
- During stressful and tough times, remain open minded and think outside the box. Don't let your emotions cloud your thinking.
- Remember, that if you are ever told "NO" it's only a stumble, not a fall. Find another way to succeed.
- Pray and listen.

Chapter 24

A New Plan for Collins Hill Athletic Club

In an effort, to grow our tennis club and to fully utilize our building, we started "The Party and Event Center" at Collins Hill Athletic Club in 2005. After the sale of Fitness International, in the spring of 2008, "The Party and Event Center" starting doing very well and demanded more of our time. We would rent the facility to the public and Chrystal would provide catering services for all types of events. We were renting our club for family reunions, birthday parties, pool parties, rehearsal dinners, and wedding receptions. We were busy for the entire year.

In early spring of 2009, Eddie Beauchamp from GGC, approached me once again, about the college purchasing our tennis club. I remember telling him I would be happy to discuss a deal; but (and this was a BIG but), I didn't want the deal to take two years to finalize like the Fitness International deal, Negotiations began. The bigger GGC grew, the more amenities were added to attract graduating seniors to attend a four-year college close to home. As tuition became more and more expensive at most of the larger colleges, GGC student registration soared. This meant more space and athletic programs were needed. In late summer 2009, rumors somehow started to swirl that the college was also looking for a tennis facility. Our members felt that the college would probably want to purchase CHAC instead of building their own. Many members at the tennis center began to cancel their memberships and our staff worried about losing their jobs. Chrystal and I decided in August 2009 to close the doors at Collins Hill Athletic Club. We needed to figure out whether the college was interested in purchasing CHAC or if we needed to reopen and start over building our business. After three months, our negotiations with the college went dormant. We decided to reopen! In a letter to our previous members we promised a new start with our programs, more tennis tournaments and drills. We added a nine-hundred-square-foot aerobics room for classes, and we would guarantee there would be someone, either a staff member or myself, available to play tennis anytime. We revamped our fitness center by adding more equipment, and I held small group training classes weekly. I personally gave free personal training sessions when requested. We provided a keyless entry service, where members could have early morning access to work out and use the facility. I guaranteed if members rejoined that Chrystal and I would be at the club to provide the best customer service possible. We reopened our club under the same name, Collins Hill Athletic Club on December 1, 2009.

When we closed the tennis center, having assumed we were selling to the college, we helped our main team members, Aubrey and Ashlie, move on to different career paths. Now we welcomed a new team to our club to help with the re-grand opening. They were Sandy Gardner, Karen Whitlock, Sue Grider, Jennifer Montgomery, Alex Ruiz, Porky Byrd, Doug Pritchard, and Kenny Hussey. We thank each of these people for all of their hard work and dedication to another successful journey.

Our previous members were very excited, and within six months, we had grown our member base to 400 members. In 2011, about one year after the club reopened, the college reached out to me again and wanted to restart negotiations. For the next twelve months, we had negotiations with the college and finally agreed to sell Collins Hill Athletic, Club (land, building and equipment) to GGC for $1.6M.

Once we had an agreement with the college, I contacted Zions Bank in hopes of negotiating a payoff for our loan. I knew after the 2008

It is NOT Impossible!

financial collapse, Zions would be anxious to release a tennis center off their books. I offered to pay my note in full within thirty days if they would give me a discount of $300,000.00, no strings attached. To my surprise within one week the bank accepted my offer. In June 2012, we closed the deal with GGC and paid off our note with Zions Bank.

Lessons Learned:

- Never hesitate to ask for something you need or want.
- When negotiating a deal, try to remember not to take it personally.
- Never feel that you are too smart to listen to other people.
- It is okay to stop and reevaluate.

Chapter 25

THE NEXT CHAPTER OF OUR LIFE!

MY WIFE, CHRYSTAL, AND I live in the Atlanta, GA, area. We love to buy and sell real estate and are always ready to travel. Finding, negotiating, and closing business deals keeps my adrenalin pumping. Exercising and sports remain part of our daily living. Chrystal has been teaching group fitness classes for thirty plus years and is still going strong. She continues to take great care of me and our three dogs. We both love spending time with my children and our families. Life is good!

This book is written about actual events that occurred in my life! I hope you enjoyed reading about my journey. It is my hope you can use my experiences as your own guide of helpful lessons. We wish you the best of luck on your path to greatness. Success is yours. Go get it!

Tim Mansour

A special note of gratitude and appreciation!

MY APPRECIATION GOES OUT TO all the special people in my life for helping to make so many of my dreams come true! God has been good to my family and me, and I thank Him for giving me the strength, passion and perseverance to be successful and happy.

A big thank you to the entire team that helped put Fitness International, Inc., ProFit Equipment Center, The Vitamin Store, The Guaranteed Weight Loss, Collins Hill Athletic Club and my other businesses on the map, and for helping to make us so successful! Daddy Joe Mansour, Isabel "Ma-bell" Mansour, Joseph Mansour III, AbbieRose Mansour, Michael Mansour, Lt. Col. Paul J. Mansour, Cherry Reynolds Tolliver, Chrystal Williams Mansour, Rocky Beebe, Carola Thomason, Ty and Sherry Ryoul, Lisa Bruce Folds, Kip Rozier, Lex Luby, Cathleen White, Theresa Fox, Ermine Martin, Mike and Mindy Greene, Wes Johnson, Donnie Floren, Helen, Ellen, Gene Mark, Tommy Duren, Pam Lane, Mike Norman, Mike Slade, Paul Cotter, Barbara Higgs, Diane Smith, Shannon Mize, Sue Nannie, Diane Lassic, Debra Johnson, Tonya Moore Arp, Cathy Stahl, Ashlie Tu, Jennifer Montgomery, Inez Klenke, Alan Najjar, Mickey Wages, Ms. Kitchens, Judy McDaniels, Aubrey Jackson, Jennifer Mendoza, Dave Matthews, Doug Pritchard, Kenny Hussey, Bill Rogers, Porky Byrd, Greg Amerson, Terhune Berne, Alex Ruiz, Sandy Gardner, Karen Whitlock, Ann Meyer and to all our great members. I know I was not able to list everyone, because there were a lot of people that worked with us over the years and I want to thank all of you for a great journey and for all the memories! I will never forget this ride.

Thank you!

Tim Mansour and family

Comments and Memorable Experiences from Family, Friends and Team Members:

Quote from Inez Klenke:

I worked at Snellville and Lawrenceville Fitness International and Collins Hills Athletic Club.

I think I worked 10 years for you, but if we include part-time it could have been 14-16 years.

No one would believe my stories! The most memorable ones are of us keeping the club open one more day and me crying! The most memorable thing I must say, is during some real hard times, when JoJo and I were stressed out, how Tim never let it get to him. He could let it roll off his back and find another solution to the problem. I never saw someone think of so many different ways to utilize what he had to improve the bottom line. I saw so many walls torn down and rebuilt to accommodate a new idea, including my many offices. I think I must have had 6 or more until I ended up in a closet, lol! Tim also was one of the best negotiators that I have ever met. He knew the value of his business and never backed down, meanwhile I was in the back throwing up! Overall, I learned a lot from Tim. That family is first, that friends are important, and that everything else is not that big of a deal. Tim, you are very dear to me. I know you will be very successful in this endeavor! May God bless you!

Inez Klenke

Quote from Shannon Mize:

I started with Tim in 1990 and worked through the 3rd quarter of 1997. I worked a couple of years at the Fitness International, Conyers location, and the remainder at Lawrenceville. One of my most memorable moments was when we were under construction in Lawrenceville. Tim came by the temporary facility and picked me up to go check on the new building's progress. The slab had been poured, the structural steel was up, and they were ready to pour the elevated slab on the second floor. I was so excited until you casually told me you hoped they approved the "construction loan" real soon!

The hours were crazy long. There were plenty of all-nighters when new equipment came in, or when we were replacing carpet, and had to move everything out and set it back up before the doors opened the next morning. It never felt like work. I always enjoyed the core group of guys, and always felt like part of the family.

Shannon Mize

Quote from Mickey Wages:

Several memorable moments stand out to me, but the most important is our friendship and respect for each other over the years. What I will never forget is helping you secure your dream of a super club in Lawrenceville, helping you save a pot full of money by refinancing Collins Hill, and remembering how proud I was to be your banker that day you won the Chamber of Commerce Small Business Person of the Year. There are other memories, but these stand out the most.

Thanks for the opportunity to contribute.

Mickey Wages

Quote from Theresa Fox:

I am not able to come up with a special story, but would love to share my wonderful memories. Fitness International was a family facility and it made exercise fun and healthier families. I could travel from club to club, and although each club had the same title, each had different personalities. Always having the same rules was a big part of our success! We had monthly meetings that brought us all together. Awesome

Christmas parties!!!! We presold Lawrenceville club by pictures and reputation. Again, what a great success! I learned a great deal from Tim and Joseph. Tim is a great businessman. Tim and Joseph are great leaders in their fields, as well as wonderful parents. I love them all, and they are a blessing in my life. Thank you.

Theresa Fox

Quote from Cathleen White:

I worked part-time/full-time at all four locations of Fitness International and in the corporate office (10 years). OMG, so many memorable moments... But I will never forget the first employee staff meetings that I attended. They had such an impact on me, sitting with people I had never met before and listening to Tim express himself with such passion and love for FITNESS INTERNATIONAL!!! He ran a tight ship, and with the help of his brother Joseph, every club was clean and the equipment was always in tip-top condition. Being able to work with his family was an incredible blessing in my life!!!!

Cathleen White

Quote from Oliver "Porky" Byrd:

I worked at Collins Hill Athletic Club, and in the past ten years that I have known Tim, several things are very evident. He is very positive in everything that he attempts. His drive is unmatched by anyone that I have ever met. I had the privilege of working with Tim as a tennis pro at Collins Hill. During this time, we became the best of friends. He and Chrystal have a great relationship, and are a positive influence on those that are privileged to know them.

Porky Byrd

Quote from Richie Mullis:

First of all, congratulations on the book, and thank you for the opportunity to share some great memories about you and our FI days! I worked at Fitness International, and my dad thought the world of you, Tim. I remember many times that he stressed to me that I better be working hard for you, because you were a good man. My dad was/is my life hero. Anyone that he liked and respected as much as he did you, deserves my respect as well.

You taught me several things about leadership in general. Excellence, hard work, discipline, professionalism...

Congrats again on your book, and I look forward to seeing you again sometime in the future!

Blessings my friend.

Richie Mullis

Quote from Ty Ryoul:

I worked at every club and in every business venture. I started working for Tim in 1987 and worked for him till 2001.

Wow, where do I start! I was only 17 when I started my employment cleaning the equipment, and I ended my career as the general manger of all four Fitness Locations. What an experience. I have too many stories and experiences to pick just one. For me, it was being part of a family. I mean, we did everything together, both professionally and personally. We worked together 7 days a week from 6 am to 9-10 pm. When we were opening a new location, there were a lot of ALL-NIGHTERS AS WELL. It was being together, working together, growing together! I truly felt I was part of something special, and was proud to be a part of such a wonderful organization. Thanks

Ty Ryoul

Quote from Trilby Minor:

I worked at Fitness International in Lawrenceville from mid 2004 to Jan. 2008, and at Collins Hill Athletic Club two summers teaching water aerobics.

I was new to Georgia, and a new mom with a baby, so getting back into teaching was a little scary. Everyone at FI was very supportive and kind. You truly were a gift from God that helped opened doors that I was unaware of at the time. Not long after I started working at FI, I went through a divorce, and the work that I had and the friends that I had made were a huge help in getting through that time. Tim and Chrystal have always been very supportive, and encouraged me to do my best, helping build me up as person as well as an instructor. I am forever grateful for being a part of such a great team!

Trilby Minor

Quote from Alan Najjar:

"There are too many memories to share about my long history with you and your family, but they all revolve around love, like, trust, and mutual respect. The first and foremost assessment in a loan decision is the borrower's **_CHARACTER._** People of character find a way to pay you back. I put my personal and professional reputation on the line in a new community bank with loans to Fitness International because I knew you and your family. I knew that you had all of Daddy Joe and Ma-bell's good traits. I knew that you and Joseph would find a way to make it work, and you did for Snellville, Stone Mountain, Conyers, Lawrenceville and later Collins Hill. You worked hard and found a way to repay every penny. I conveyed my trust and belief in you and your business to Jim Pack and Mickey Wages at Gwinnett Federal, and they took your banking relationship to the next level. The Collins Hill tennis facility was another example of your successful execution of a business plan. Again, you repaid every penny.

Yesterday was Donna's 62nd birthday, and I will always remember when you, your family, and your staff opened the doors to the Snellville Hall Event Center to host 100+ guests at Donna's 40th birthday party. We are closer than family, and our relationship has no expiration date.

I am proud of you, and love you like a brother.

Alan N.

Quote from Greg Amerson:

Worked at Collins Hill Athletic Club for three-plus years as a Tennis Pro

"What I remember the most, really, was how you and Joseph made me feel a part of the family. I felt like one of your brothers. The trip to Las Vegas and all the great times at the club can never be forgotten. The great academy that we created produced a professional player as well as many college players. Look at what we did in only three short years"

You showed me what success and hard work looks like. Thanks!

Greg

www.ingramcontent.com/pod-product-compliance
Lightning Source LLC
Chambersburg PA
CBHW070114080526
44586CB00013B/1296